DATE DUE

DE 17 '05			

HYGIENE

GENERAL EDITORS

Dale C. Garell, M.D.
Medical Director, California Children Services, Department of Health Services, County of Los Angeles
Associate Dean for Curriculum; Clinical Professor, Department of Pediatrics & Family Medicine, University of Southern California School of Medicine
Former President, Society for Adolescent Medicine

Solomon H. Snyder, M.D.
Distinguished Service Professor of Neuroscience, Pharmacology, and Psychiatry, Johns Hopkins University School of Medicine
Former President, Society for Neuroscience
Albert Lasker Award in Medical Research, 1978

CONSULTING EDITORS

Robert W. Blum, M.D., Ph.D.
Professor and Director, Division of General Pediatrics and Adolescent Health, University of Minnesota

Charles E. Irwin, Jr., M.D.
Professor of Pediatrics; Director, Division of Adolescent Medicine, University of California, San Francisco

Lloyd J. Kolbe, Ph.D.
Director of the Division of Adolescent and School Health, Center for Chronic Disease Prevention and Health Promotion, Centers for Disease Control

Jordan J. Popkin
Former Director, Division of Federal Employee Occupational Health, U.S. Public Health Service Region I

Joseph L. Rauh, M.D.
Professor of Pediatrics and Medicine, Adolescent Medicine, Children's Hospital Medical Center, Cincinnati
Former President, Society for Adolescent Medicine

THE ENCYCLOPEDIA OF
H E A L T H

THE HEALTHY BODY

Dale C. Garell, M.D. · General Editor

HYGIENE

Don Nardo

Introduction by C. Everett Koop, M.D., Sc.D.

former Surgeon General, U. S. Public Health Service

CHELSEA HOUSE PUBLISHERS

New York · Philadelphia

.TH *is to provide general information in*
psychology, and related medical issues.
ed to take the place of the professional
advice of a physician or other health care professional.

CHELSEA HOUSE PUBLISHERS
EDITORIAL DIRECTOR   Richard Rennert
EXECUTIVE MANAGING EDITOR   Karyn Gullen Browne
EXECUTIVE EDITOR   Sean Dolan
COPY CHIEF   Philip Koslow
PICTURE EDITOR   Adrian G. Allen
ART DIRECTOR   Nora Wertz
MANUFACTURING DIRECTOR   Gerald Levine
SYSTEMS MANAGER   Lindsey Ottman
PRODUCTION COORDINATOR   Marie Claire Cebrián-Ume

The Encyclopedia of Health
SENIOR EDITOR   Kenneth W. Lane

Staff for HYGIENE
COPY EDITOR   Danielle Janusz
EDITORIAL ASSISTANT   Mary B. Sisson
PICTURE RESEARCHER   Sandy Jones
DESIGNER   M. Cambraia Magalhaes

First Printing
1   3   5   7   9   8   6   4   2

Library of Congress Cataloging-in-Publication Data

Nardo, Don. 1947–
   Hygiene/by Don Nardo; introduction by C. Everett Koop.
      p. cm.— (The Encyclopedia of health)
   Includes bibliographical references and index.
Summary: An examination of the importance of hygiene, problems associated with
maintaining proper hygiene, and means of its effective practice.
ISBN 0-7910-0020-6
      0-7910-0460-0 (pbk.)
   1. Public health—Juvenile literature. 2.   Hygiene—Juvenile literature. 3. Sanita-
tion—Juvenile literature. [1. Cleanliness. 2. Health. 3. Public health. 4. Sanitation.]
I. Title. II. Series.
RA432.N37 1993   92-32086
   614 — dc20   CIP
                                                                              AC

CONTENTS

THE ENCYCLOPEDIA OF HEALTH

THE HEALTHY BODY

The Circulatory System
Dental Health
The Digestive System
The Endocrine System
Exercise
Genetics & Heredity
The Human Body: An Overview
Hygiene
The Immune System
Memory & Learning
The Musculoskeletal System
The Nervous System
Nutrition
The Reproductive System
The Respiratory System
The Senses
Sleep
Speech & Hearing
Sports Medicine
Vision
Vitamins & Minerals

THE LIFE CYCLE

Adolescence
Adulthood
Aging
Childhood
Death & Dying
The Family
Friendship & Love
Pregnancy & Birth

MEDICAL ISSUES

Careers in Health Care
Environmental Health
Folk Medicine
Health Care Delivery
Holistic Medicine
Medical Ethics
Medical Fakes & Frauds
Medical Technology
Medicine & the Law
Occupational Health
Public Health

PSYCHOLOGICAL DISORDERS AND THEIR TREATMENT

Anxiety & Phobias
Child Abuse
Compulsive Behavior
Delinquency & Criminal Behavior
Depression
Diagnosing & Treating Mental Illness
Eating Habits & Disorders
Learning Disabilities
Mental Retardation
Personality Disorders
Schizophrenia
Stress Management
Suicide

MEDICAL DISORDERS AND THEIR TREATMENT

AIDS
Allergies
Alzheimer's Disease
Arthritis
Birth Defects
Cancer
The Common Cold
Diabetes
Emergency Medicine
Gynecological Disorders
Headaches
The Hospital
Kidney Disorders
Medical Diagnosis
The Mind-Body Connection
Mononucleosis and Other Infectious Diseases
Nuclear Medicine
Organ Transplants
Pain
Physical Handicaps
Poisons & Toxins
Prescription & OTC Drugs
Sexually Transmitted Diseases
Skin Disorders
Stroke & Heart Disease
Substance Abuse
Tropical Medicine

PREVENTION AND EDUCATION: THE KEYS TO GOOD HEALTH

C. Everett Koop, M.D., Sc.D.
former Surgeon General,
U.S. Public Health Service

The issue of health education has received particular attention in recent years because of the presence of AIDS in the news. But our response to this particular tragedy points up a number of broader issues that doctors, public health officials, educators, and the public face. In particular, it points up the necessity for sound health education for citizens of all ages.

Over the past 25 years this country has been able to bring about dramatic declines in the death rates for heart disease, stroke, accidents, and for people under the age of 45, cancer. Today, Americans generally eat better and take better care of themselves than ever before. Thus, with the help of modern science and technology, they have a better chance of surviving serious—even catastrophic—illnesses. That's the good news.

But, like every phonograph record, there's a flip side, and one with special significance for young adults. According to a report issued in 1979 by Dr. Julius Richmond, my predecessor as Surgeon General, Americans aged 15 to 24 had a higher death rate in 1979 than they did 20 years earlier. The causes: violent death and injury, alcohol and drug abuse, unwanted pregnancies, and sexually transmitted diseases. Adolescents are particularly vulnerable because they are beginning to explore their own sexuality and perhaps to experiment with drugs. The need for educating young people is critical, and the price of neglect is high.

Yet even for the population as a whole, our health is still far from what it could be. Why? A 1974 Canadian government report attributed all death and disease to four broad elements: inadequacies in the health care system, behavioral factors or unhealthy life-styles, environmental hazards, and human biological factors.

To be sure, there are diseases that are still beyond the control of even our advanced medical knowledge and techniques. And despite yearnings that are as old as the human race itself, there is no "fountain of youth" to ward off aging and death. Still, there is a solution to many of the problems that undermine sound health. In a word, that solution is prevention. Prevention, which includes health promotion and education, saves lives, improves the quality of life, and in the long run, saves money.

In the United States, organized public health activities and preventive medicine have a long history. Important milestones in this country or foreign breakthroughs adopted in the United States include the improvement of sanitary procedures and the development of pasteurized milk in the late 19th century and the introduction in the mid-20th century of effective vaccines against polio, measles, German measles, mumps, and other once-rampant diseases. Internationally, organized public health efforts began on a wide-scale basis with the International Sanitary Conference of 1851, to which 12 nations sent representatives. The World Health Organization, founded in 1948, continues these efforts under the aegis of the United Nations, with particular emphasis on combating communicable diseases and the training of health care workers.

Despite these accomplishments, much remains to be done in the field of prevention. For too long, we have had a medical care system that is science- and technology-based, focused, essentially, on illness and mortality. It is now patently obvious that both the social and the economic costs of such a system are becoming insupportable.

Implementing prevention—and its corollaries, health education and promotion—is the job of several groups of people.

First, the medical and scientific professions need to continue basic scientific research, and here we are making considerable progress. But increased concern with prevention will also have a decided impact on how primary care doctors practice medicine. With a shift to health-based rather than morbidity-based medicine, the role of the "new physician" will include a healthy dose of patient education.

Second, practitioners of the social and behavioral sciences—psychologists, economists, city planners—along with lawyers, business leaders, and government officials—must solve the practical and ethical dilemmas confronting us: poverty, crime, civil rights, literacy, education, employment, housing, sanitation, environmental protection, health care delivery systems, and so forth. All of these issues affect public health.

Third is the public at large. We'll consider that very important group in a moment.

Fourth, and the linchpin in this effort, is the public health profession—doctors, epidemiologists, teachers—who must harness the professional expertise of the first two groups and the common sense and cooperation of the third, the public. They must define the problems statistically and qualitatively and then help us set priorities for finding the solutions.

To a very large extent, improving those statistics is the responsibility of every individual. So let's consider more specifically what the role of the individual should be and why health education is so important to that role. First, and most obvious, individuals can protect themselves from illness and injury and thus minimize their need for professional medical care. They can eat nutritious food; get adequate exercise; avoid tobacco, alcohol, and drugs; and take prudent steps to avoid accidents. The proverbial "apple a day keeps the doctor away" is not so far from the truth, after all.

Second, individuals should actively participate in their own medical care. They should schedule regular medical and dental checkups. Should they develop an illness or injury, they should know when to treat themselves and when to seek professional help. To gain the maximum benefit from any medical treatment that they do require, individuals must become partners in that treatment. For instance, they should understand the effects and side effects of medications. I counsel young physicians that there is no such thing as too much information when talking with patients. But the corollary is the patient must know enough about the nuts and bolts of the healing process to understand what the doctor is telling him or her. That is at least partially the patient's responsibility.

Education is equally necessary for us to understand the ethical and public policy issues in health care today. Sometimes individuals will encounter these issues in making decisions about their own treatment or that of family members. Other citizens may encounter them as jurors in medical malpractice cases. But we all become involved, indirectly, when we elect our public officials, from school board members to the president. Should surrogate parenting be legal? To what extent is drug testing desirable, legal, or necessary? Should there be public funding for family planning, hospitals, various types of medical research, and other medical care for the indigent? How should we allocate scant technological resources, such as kidney dialysis and organ transplants? What is the proper role of government in protecting the rights of patients?

What are the broad goals of public health in the United States today? In 1980, the Public Health Service issued a report aptly entitled *Promoting Health—Preventing Disease: Objectives for the Nation*. This report expressed its goals in terms of mortality and in terms of intermediate goals in education and health improvement. It identified 15 major concerns: controlling high blood pressure; improving family planning; improving pregnancy care and infant health; increasing the rate of immunization; controlling sexually transmitted diseases; controlling the presence of toxic agents and radiation in the environment; improving occupational safety and health; preventing accidents; promoting water fluoridation and dental health; controlling infectious diseases; decreasing smoking; decreasing alcohol and drug abuse; improving nutrition; promoting physical fitness and exercise; and controlling stress and violent behavior.

For healthy adolescents and young adults (ages 15 to 24), the specific goal was a 20% reduction in deaths, with a special focus on motor vehicle injuries and alcohol and drug abuse. For adults (ages 25 to 64), the aim was 25% fewer deaths, with a concentration on heart attacks, strokes, and cancers.

Smoking is perhaps the best example of how individual behavior can have a direct impact on health. Today, cigarette smoking is recognized as the single most important preventable cause of death in our society. It is responsible for more cancers and more cancer deaths than any other known agent; is a prime risk factor for heart and blood vessel disease, chronic bronchitis, and emphysema; and is a frequent cause of complications in pregnancies and of babies born prematurely, underweight, or with potentially fatal respiratory and cardiovascular problems.

Since the release of the Surgeon General's first report on smoking in 1964, the proportion of adult smokers has declined substantially, from 43% in 1965 to 30.5% in 1985. Since 1965, 37 million people have quit smoking. Although there is still much work to be done if we are to become a "smoke-free society," it is heartening to note that public health and public education efforts—such as warnings on cigarette packages and bans on broadcast advertising—have already had significant effects.

In 1835, Alexis de Tocqueville, a French visitor to America, wrote, "In America the passion for physical well-being is general." Today, as then, health and fitness are front-page items. But with the greater scientific and technological resources now available to us, we are in a far stronger position to make good health care available to everyone. And with the greater technological threats to us as we approach the 21st century, the need to do so is more urgent than ever before. Comprehensive information about basic biology, preventive medicine, medical and surgical treatments, and related ethical and public policy issues can help you arm yourself with the knowledge you need to be healthy throughout your life.

FOREWORD

Dale C. Garell, M.D.

Advances in our understanding of health and disease during the 20th century have been truly remarkable. Indeed, it could be argued that modern health care is one of the greatest accomplishments in all of human history. In the early 20th century, improvements in sanitation, water treatment, and sewage disposal reduced death rates and increased longevity. Previously untreatable illnesses can now be managed with antibiotics, immunizations, and modern surgical techniques. Discoveries in the fields of immunology, genetic diagnosis, and organ transplantation are revolutionizing the prevention and treatment of disease. Modern medicine is even making inroads against cancer and heart disease, two of the leading causes of death in the United States.

Although there is much to be proud of, medicine continues to face enormous challenges. Science has vanquished diseases such as smallpox and polio, but new killers, most notably AIDS, confront us. Moreover, we now victimize ourselves with what some have called "diseases of choice," or those brought on by drug and alcohol abuse, bad eating habits, and mismanagement of the stresses and strains of contemporary life. The very technology that is doing so much to prolong life has brought with it previously unimaginable ethical dilemmas related to issues of death and dying. The rising cost of health care is a matter of central concern to us all. And violence in the form of automobile accidents, homicide, and suicide remains the major killer of young adults.

In the past, most people were content to leave health care and medical treatment in the hands of professionals. But since the 1960s, the consumer of medical care—that is, the patient—has assumed an increasingly central role in the management of his or her own health. There has also been a new emphasis placed on prevention: People are recognizing that their own actions can help prevent many of the conditions that have caused death and disease in the past. This accounts for the growing commitment to good nutrition and regular exercise, for the increasing number of people who are choosing not to smoke, and for a new moderation in people's drinking habits.

People want to know more about themselves and their own health. They are curious about their body: its anatomy, physiology, and biochemistry. They want to keep up with rapidly evolving medical technologies and procedures. They are willing to educate themselves about common disorders and diseases so that they can be full partners in their own health care.

THE ENCYCLOPEDIA OF HEALTH is designed to provide the basic knowledge that readers will need if they are to take significant responsibility for their own health. It is also meant to serve as a frame of reference for further study and exploration. The encyclopedia is divided into five subsections: The Healthy Body; The Life Cycle; Medical Disorders & Their Treatment; Psychological Disorders & Their Treatment; and Medical Issues. For each topic covered by the encyclopedia, we present the essential facts about the relevant biology; the symptoms, diagnosis, and treatment of common diseases and disorders; and ways in which you can prevent or reduce the severity of health problems when that is possible. The encyclopedia also projects what may lie ahead in the way of future treatment or prevention strategies.

The broad range of topics and issues covered in the encyclopedia reflects that human health encompasses physical, psychological, social, environmental, and spiritual well-being. Just as the mind and the body are inextricably linked, so, too, is the individual an integral part of the wider world that comprises his or her family, society, and environment. To discuss health in its broadest aspect it is necessary to explore the many ways in which it is connected to such fields as law, social science, public policy, economics, and even religion. And so, the encyclopedia is meant to be a bridge between science, medical technology, the world at large, and you. I hope that it will inspire you to pursue in greater depth particular areas of interest and that you will take advantage of the suggestions for further reading and the lists of resources and organizations that can provide additional information.

HYGIENE

CHAPTER 1

LIVING IN FILTH— LACK OF HYGIENE IN PAST AGES

In 1665, an outbreak of the plague in London killed tens of thousands of people. Major outbreaks of the plague swept through Europe as a result of a lack of public and personal hygiene.

Doctors and health care professionals broadly define *hygiene* as the application of science to the preservation of good health and the prevention of disease. Because they help maintain good health, such factors as personal cleanliness, good diet and nutrition, and the avoidance of unhealthy habits, such as smoking, are important aspects of hygiene, as are public water purification, sewage systems, and pest control, all of which help eliminate the threat of infectious diseases.

Most people living in modern, affluent countries such as the United States take for granted clean running water, government inspection of food, garbage and sewage disposal systems, and vaccinations against infectious diseases. But these and other general health measures are relatively recent developments. Many people view life in past eras as having been idyllic, romantic, or quaint, and refer nostalgically to the "good old days." It is easy to remember only the pleasant aspects of those days and overlook the fact that there were no flush toilets or public sewers, no clean water flowing out of the kitchen tap, and no way to stop the spread of deadly diseases. Before the 20th century, there were few hygienic practices, either public or private, anywhere in the world. As a result, most people lived in horrendously filthy, unsanitary conditions that promoted widespread sickness, disease, and misery.

The largest single factor contributing to the general lack of hygiene was ignorance. Most people were uneducated and superstitious, relying on the knowledge passed on to them by relatives, friends, and priests to get by in everyday life. They knew little or nothing about the

In major cities of the Western Hemisphere, poor sanitary conditions persisted well into the 19th century. Rats, which carried many diseases including the plague, presented a serious problem even within hospitals, as in this illustration of patients in New York City's Bellevue Hospital.

workings of nature. Even the so-called scientists explained natural laws in terms of the whims of the gods and by other folklore until only a few hundred years ago. For thousands of years, there were no scientific methods or devices with which to study natural phenomena and processes.

The Spread of Disease

This lack of scientific knowledge and instruments for studying nature had serious health consequences. For instance, until the 1600s there were no microscopes powerful enough to reveal the existence of germs, and even then no one connected these tiny creatures with disease. As a result, the chances of contracting a disease and dying from it were much greater than they are today.

People did not know that trillions of germs teemed everywhere around them, in the air they breathed, in the water they drank, in the food they ate, in the soil they tilled, and even on their own bodies. Many of these germs were harmless, but others were dangerous, and both kinds traveled easily from person to person, house to house, and village to village. Consequently, throughout history there were periodic outbreaks of crippling or deadly diseases, such as leprosy, yellow fever, and typhus. Epidemics of measles, cholera, smallpox, and other maladies regularly wiped out thousands, even millions, of people at a time. People in every culture came to accept the death and misery that accompanied these plagues as expected facts of life.

Perhaps the most dramatic example of epidemic disease in history was the terrifying outbreak of bubonic plague that occurred in Europe in the 14th century. Also called the "Black Death," the plague swept from town to town and country to country, spreading fear, misery, and social chaos as well as death. Although different estimates have been given for the plague's overall death toll, it may have killed as many as 25 million people, nearly one-third of Europe's population at the time. The Black Death struck suddenly and did not discriminate between rich and poor, noble and common-born, devout and faithless. No one was safe from the disease, and every family was visited at least once by a death cart hauling victims to mass graves.

The widespread lack of hygiene and the casual acceptance of various kinds of animal pests were what made the bubonic plague so devastating. The cause of the plague was a species of bacteria that infested fleas, which in turn, infested rats and other animals. The rats, carrying the fleas, brought the contagion into human habitations.

In 14th-century Europe, it was a rare house or city block that did not support at least a modest population of rats, mice, or other vermin. With so many millions of rodents and humans cohabitating, the plague spread with terrible swiftness. At the time, the way the plague spread was completely unknown because people knew nothing about the germ theory of disease, which was not formulated until the 19th century. Disease was commonly viewed as a punishment brought on by God. According to prevailing thought in 14th-century Europe, the spread of an epidemic through an entire town or country generally meant that God believed that town or country to be corrupt. In the case of the Black Death, most people assumed that humanity was finally paying the price for centuries of sin, immorality, and ungodliness.

According to priests and other church officials, the only way people could halt the plague was to beg for God's forgiveness. But while many people prayed, the disease continued to take its ghastly toll, and some adopted the fatalistic view that God had decided to abandon humanity once and for all. In a desperate attempt to get God to reconsider, some people joined groups of religious fanatics known as flagellants. They journeyed from town to town, telling people that the only way to get God's attention and forgiveness was to punish themselves for the accumulated sins of humanity. The flagellants publicly stripped, then beat themselves and each other with spike-tipped whips until they collapsed, exhausted and bleeding, in the streets. Their objective was to convince everyone in Europe to join their crusade. They believed that God would eventually see their sacrifice and end the plague. Whether God actually intervened and lifted the epidemic is a matter of faith. Scientists maintain that the disease ran its course naturally and subsided after a few years, although there were smaller outbreaks in Europe and other parts of the world in subsequent centuries.

Streets Filled with Manure

That so many people in ancient times contracted and died of such diseases as the bubonic plague is hardly surprising, considering the deplorable conditions in which most people existed. For example, it was fairly common for families to live in stone or wooden shacks, with as many as 9 or 10 people crammed into one or two small rooms. When it rained, the cold, earthen floors in many of these homes became damp and soggy. Mud from the outside, as well as decaying scraps of food and other refuse from the inside, littered the areas where people ate and slept.

The situation was not much better for those who lived in larger, sturdier houses with wooden floors. There was so much filth in public areas that some was bound to be tracked into homes. Most people threw their garbage into the streets, walkways, and gardens, and germs bred in the garbage as it rotted. People and animals then walked on this litter and carried contagion into houses via their shoes or bare feet.

The streets were also filled with human and animal wastes. Animals regularly left piles of manure in the streets, yards, and stables, where people picked it up on their shoes as they walked. Many people kept buckets or barrels in their houses for their own wastes and allowed these containers to fill up, after which they dumped them into street gutters, backyard manure piles, or even into ponds and streams. Those with separate outhouses also dumped their accumulated wastes into piles. Various kinds of insects, some of which are carriers of disease, bred in these noxious mounds. To make matters worse, the sun often dried the manure into a powder, which was picked up by the wind and deposited over towns and homes and into open windows.

Very little clean water could be found anywhere. Commonly, all of the people in a town or neighborhood used water from the same stream or well for drinking, washing clothes, and other needs. Most people were not careful about keeping the water clean, and it often became contaminated by garbage, manure, and other litter. Animals, both domestic and wild, drank from or walked through the water, picking

Through most of human history, human and animal wastes filled the streets of villages and cities, creating breeding grounds for disease. Although developed nations have largely eliminated this problem, it remains a serious threat in the world's less developed regions.

up germs from it while polluting it with still more filth and disease-causing germs.

Lack of hygiene was especially apparent in food habits. There was no scientific knowledge about proper nutrition, and poor diet often led to vitamin deficiencies and other physical problems. The ways in which food was prepared were also frequently unhealthy. For instance, people often used unwashed knives to slaughter cattle, sheep, and other animals, unaware that they might be spreading disease. Afterward, they stored the meat in unsanitary places, open to infestation by parasites and germs of all kinds. Often, people did not thoroughly clean their dishes, cups, and knives after eating, and the remaining crusts of decaying food became further breeding grounds for disease-causing germs. It was also common practice to eat vegetables and fruits unwashed, sometimes after insects and rodents had nibbled at them, thus infecting the eaters with any diseases carried by these animals. Because refrigeration had not yet been invented, food did not keep very long before it spoiled. No one realized that germs were what caused food to spoil—germs that often brought outbreaks of food poisoning to an unwary populace.

Diseases also spread via the decaying corpses of humans and animals. In ancient and medieval times, people matter-of-factly handled human corpses with their bare hands while moving and preparing them for burial, a practice that enabled disease to travel from the dead to the living. Sometimes, people threw diseased bodies into lakes or streams, unaware that by doing so they were contaminating the water.

A Lack of Personal Cleanliness

During most of the thousands of years in which human beings have lived on earth, slovenly personal bathing and grooming habits have often promoted the spread of sickness and disease. Before modern times, bathing was not a regular habit in many parts of the world, and in some places is still not done regularly. There are some notable exceptions to this in the historical record. For example, the ancient Egyptians, especially the noble and wealthy classes, appear to have bathed fairly frequently. They also used special ointments and deodorants after bathing, much as people do today.

According to tradition, Moses was raised as an Egyptian prince and passed on Egyptian cleanliness rituals to the Hebrews when he led them out of Egypt. From then on, Hebrew worshipers washed their clothes to purify themselves before hearing the word of God, and Hebrew religious leaders cleansed their hands and feet before going near an altar. The Hebrews also had unusually strict dietary habits in comparison to other ancient peoples. For example, by a law laid down in the Old Testament, they were forbidden to eat pork. Pork often contains such parasites as tapeworms, and by following this dietary practice both the ancient Hebrews and modern Jews who have continued the practice have rarely suffered from parasite-related problems.

The Romans, too, put a great deal of emphasis on cleaning themselves, as evidenced by the number of public baths in Roman cities. These were usually fairly large buildings with many interconnected rooms and chambers. People passed from one room to another, rubbing themselves with oil in one, steaming themselves in another, and taking hot and cold baths in still other chambers. Men and women did not bathe together. Instead, they either bathed at separate times of the day or in different buildings.

But the hygienic practices of the Hebrews and Romans were the exception rather than the rule. In most ancient cultures, personal cleanliness was largely neglected and sometimes even frowned upon. Poor hygiene was especially prevalent in medieval Europe, partly because of religious attitudes. The early Christian church, for example, looked upon the Roman baths not as institutions for promoting hygiene but as havens for nudity, lust, and sexual depravity. By the sixth century the Roman Catholic church already frowned on bathing, prompting Saint Benedict to command, "To those that are well, and especially to the young, bathing shall seldom be permitted."

Jailed for Taking a Bath

Perpetuating this negative attitude toward washing, the Christian monk Saint Francis of Assisi preached that people should show their devotion and love for God by never bathing at all. Many people in Europe followed his and other church teachings quite literally, refusing to wash under any circumstances. Spain's Queen Isabella, who granted Columbus his ships, bragged that she had bathed only twice in her life, the first time when she was born, and the second just prior to her marriage. Some historians jokingly remark that during the Middle Ages, Europe went a thousand years without a bath.

This societal phobia about bathing continued well into early modern times, influencing customs of personal cleanliness in colonial America. In early Pennsylvania and Virginia, for example, town elders attempted to discourage people from displaying their nude bodies by introducing strict written laws banning or limiting bathing. One of these laws ordained that a person who took a bath more than once a month was to be jailed.

Often, it was not laws, customs, or personal likes and dislikes that dictated cleanliness. Unfortunately, the proper means of keeping clean were not always readily available. Dr. V. W. Greene of the Ben Gurion Medical School in Beersheba, Israel, who has studied the spread of

One of the diseases that continues to occur in parts of the world without modern hygienic conveniences is cholera. Caused by a species of bacteria that spreads from one human being to another in sewage-tainted food and water, cholera causes the body to lose massive quantities of fluids and nutrients, as in the case of this infant in India.

diseases, points out that in early Britain "There was no running water, streams were cold and polluted, heating fuel was expensive, and soap was hard to get. There just weren't facilities for personal hygiene. Cleanliness wasn't a part of the folk culture."

The consequences of this general lack of hygiene were sometimes disastrous, because the dirtier people were, the easier it was for disease germs to spread. According to Greene, "Europeans and Americans lived in wretched filth, and many died young of associated diseases." Such maladies as dysentery and infant diarrhea killed millions of children in Europe in the 19th century alone. Many diseases are transmitted by feces, urine, and other secretions on contaminated hands or other objects. Greene points out that the greatest cause of fatal infant diarrhea came from mothers who went to the toilet, did not wash their hands, and passed along intestinal bacteria to their babies.

To make matters worse, filthy bodies were more often than not also infested with bugs, including head lice, bedbugs, and fleas. Beyond being irritating pests, many of these unwanted but frequent visitors to most households carried deadly diseases. Lice, for example, carried relapsing fever, and fleas transported bubonic plague. Germ-infected pests also infested clothing, bed linens, and pets, making it all the more difficult for people to escape the ravages of disease.

Humanity Begins To Clean Up Its Act

It was during the 19th century that major changes in public and personal hygiene occurred in industrialized countries such as the United States, the United Kingdom, and many European nations. A significant example was the Act for the Relief of Sick and Disabled Seamen, passed by the U.S. Congress in 1798, which provided for health care for sailors and seamen. This and other related acts led to the establishment of the U.S. Public Health Service in 1870. The job of the Public Health Service and its branch, the National Institutes of Health (NIH), is to study the spread of disease and other health-related factors.

Perhaps the most important health-related event prior to the 20th century was the confirmation of the germ theory of disease by Germany's Robert Koch and France's Louis Pasteur in the 1860s and

By identifying bacteria and other germs as major causes of human disease, Louis Pasteur (1822–95) helped blaze the trail for the prevention and control of many such illnesses.

1870s. By linking germs with disease, scientists were able to find ways of controlling the growth and spread of germs. Doctors and nurses began washing their hands before examining patients, and hospitals found techniques to sterilize instruments and operating rooms. Pasteur also discovered that boiling wine and milk destroyed harmful bacteria in these drinks, and the process, called pasteurization in his honor, quickly became a standard procedure. In addition, vaccines and antibiotics, two types of germ-fighting medicines, were developed, enabling doctors to save the lives of millions of disease victims.

There were other sweeping improvements in public cleanliness. Many cities introduced regular garbage collections and built sewers to remove human and animal wastes, resulting in cleaner streets and less tracking of contagion into homes. After 1854, when Dr. John Snow demonstrated that cholera epidemics in London were caused by contaminated water from city wells, many cities constructed water purification plants and built networks of pipes to carry clean water to homes and businesses.

While these changes were being implemented, personal hygienic habits also improved. Bathing began to make a comeback in the mid-1800s when Great Britain's Edwin Chadwick and other public officials noted that filth bred nothing but disease and poverty. Great Britain opened public bathhouses and washhouses in the 1850s, providing more than 1 million baths a year at a cost of 1 million pounds. But the money seemed well spent, for as science historian Dorothy Porter explains, "By that point it was clear that disease and related destitution were costing England much, much more." In the first quarter of the 19th century, many people began installing bathtubs in their houses and, by the turn of the century, popular demand prompted builders in the United States and many parts of Europe to regularly include modern-style bathrooms in new homes. Eventually, large numbers of people began to recognize the health benefits of regular visits to dentists, proper nutrition, and physical exercise.

These advances did not happen by accident. The major reason for the extensive improvement in hygiene during the 19th and 20th centuries was that people and governments applied scientific knowledge and discoveries to their everyday lives. Scientists and doctors systematically studied the factors that contributed to both sickness and health and the results were clear: the good old days had not been so good after all; living in filth was no match for good hygiene.

CHAPTER 2

FIGHTING COMMUNICABLE DISEASES

In their efforts to prevent the spread of infectious disease, many American cities attempted to eradicate the animals, insects, and other agents that spread such disease to humans. One such preventive effort was a rat patrol, shown here in Philadelphia in 1914.

One of the major impediments to good hygiene is poor health caused by disease. There are two broad categories of disease: communicable and noncommunicable. The second will be discussed in chapter 6. The first category, communicable or infectious diseases, consists of illnesses that can spread from one living creature to another. These diseases are caused by microorganisms, or germs—tiny living cells that cannot be seen with the naked eye. Germs spread through the environment via air, soil, water, and food. Once inside a larger living creature, such as a human being, disease-causing germs multiply and impair bodily functions in one or more ways.

Parasites—which are usually small living creatures that enter the body of a larger creature, or host, and live by consuming its tissues and nutrients—also cause communicable diseases. Doctors, hospitals, and public health organizations constantly struggle to identify and diagnose the diseases caused by germs and parasites, as well as to find ways to treat and eradicate these diseases.

Germs and Parasites

As discussed in the preceding chapter, for most of recorded history, the causes of disease were unknown. Then, in the 19th century, such pioneers in medical research as Louis Pasteur and Robert Koch helped found the science of microbiology, the study of microscopic creatures. In Koch and Pasteur's time, scientists recognized four general categories of germs: bacteria, fungi, protozoans, and algae.

They learned that algae, which thrive in water by converting sunlight into nutrients through the process known as *photosynthesis*, are rarely disease-producing. But the researchers also found that many of the germs in the other three categories did cause disease. Over the course of several decades, scientists also proved the existence of a fifth category of germs—viruses—and learned much more about other kinds of germs.

They learned, for example, that bacteria are relatively simple, single-celled organisms that reproduce by dividing in half, a process called *fission*, and multiply very rapidly. One of the most important qualities of bacteria is that they can live in a wide variety of environments and temperatures. Some bacteria need oxygen to survive, while others live without oxygen.

Some bacteria are harmless, living within and even benefiting the bodies of animals and humans, but others cause diseases, such as cholera, leprosy, and anthrax. Some fungi, such as mushrooms, are not germs. Other fungi, including several kinds of the single-celled fungi called *yeasts*, can and do infect humans and are considered germs. Oval shaped and much larger than bacteria, yeasts are responsible for vaginal infections in humans. Among the other fungal infections that affect humans are athlete's foot and ringworm (which is not a type of worm at all), but some fungi also cause much more serious and even fatal infections of the lungs and other parts of the human body. Some fungi reproduce by releasing spores, which are spread by winds and water, as well as on or in the bodies of humans and animals.

Protozoans are large, single-celled organisms with relatively complex internal structures, including a cell *nucleus* much like that found in the cells of higher animals and plants. Protozoans reproduce when their nuclei divide, a process called *mitosis*. They live in water and other liquids and move almost constantly. Some push or pull themselves along with tiny pseudopods, or false feet, which they extend from their single cells. Others move with the aid of whiplike flagellae that extend outside their cells. Other protozoans have tiny, hairlike appendages called cilia, which surround their cells and move in unison to propel them through their environment much as oars propel a boat. Protozoans often live as parasites in higher life forms, and cause such diseases as malaria and sleeping sickness.

Viruses are very different from the other types of germs. They are, for example, hundreds and sometimes thousands of times smaller than the other types of germs. Because of this, scientists must use very powerful specialized microscopes to see them. Viruses are also not cellular like bacteria, fungi, and protozoa, instead consisting of two simple kinds of substances—nucleic acid and protein—that can reproduce only inside the living cells of other organisms. Viruses are therefore parasites that live within these other cells, often causing serious diseases such as smallpox and rabies.

Other germs may also penetrate into the cells of another organism, damaging them from within, or may reside within the body of the larger organism but outside its cells. Many bacteria give off poisons called *toxins*, which may destroy the cells of their host or travel through the host within its bloodstream or other fluids. Many toxins cause serious physical effects, such as fever, abnormalities of the heart, and diarrhea. Some small multicellular organisms also cause communicable diseases by passing from the body of one creature to another through infected food or water. Among these multicellular parasites are the flatworms and *roundworms*, which often reproduce and grow within the stomach, intestines, and other organs of their host. Tapeworms, hookworms, and pinworms are among the varieties of multicellular parasites that cause human disease.

Tracking Down Clues to the Spread of Disease

In order to safeguard human health, doctors and other health care professionals and health-related organizations constantly study and track the spread of disease-causing germs and parasites. In the United States, two branches of the Public Health Service perform these duties. The National Institutes of Health, centered in Bethesda, Maryland, just outside Washington, D.C., conducts research that identifies and studies diseases and their causes. The Centers for Disease Control, or CDC,

Insects are major agents in the spread of several infectious diseases. One such disease is malaria, which remains a serious problem in many tropical regions of the world and is spread by mosquitoes belonging to several species, including Anopheles quadrimaculatus, *shown here.*

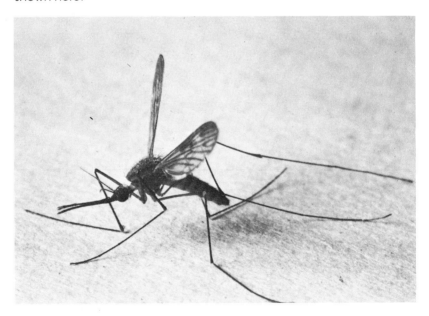

located in Atlanta, Georgia, tracks diseases both to find out how they spread and to contain them before they become dangerous epidemics.

Many diseases, such as bubonic plague, have decimated large populations in the past, and some of these diseases remain a threat, especially in poor, heavily populated areas with inadequate sanitation facilities. Therefore, doctors who work for organizations responsible for public hygiene, such as the CDC, must be constantly vigilant in order to check the spread of disease. Some of these doctors specialize in the science of *epidemiology*, the systematic study of disease epidemics.

These epidemiologists are, in a sense, disease detectives who track down clues to the various ways in which germs spread disease. Epidemiologists learned from the beginning that explaining how a particular disease spreads did not close the book on that disease, even when a cure for the disease was known. There could be new outbreaks of a disease at any time, and these outbreaks might occur in areas where people did not know about safety measures to keep the disease from spreading. In other cases, the germs responsible for the disease might reach their victims in some previously unrecognized way.

For example, scientists had shown in the 1800s that cholera was caused by bacteria that contaminated water. They demonstrated that ensuring the cleanliness of drinking-water supplies greatly reduced the incidence of cholera but did not completely eliminate the threat that it posed. There were serious epidemics in 1899 and 1923 that swept large areas of the world. Doctors learned to treat the disease and even to make people immune to *Vibrio cholerae*, the bacteria that caused cholera, for up to six months, but that did not prevent the disease from returning. Another serious outbreak began in the 1970s, killing 75,000 people worldwide in 1978 alone.

Modern Disease Fighters

To prevent further epidemics, physicians now track such diseases as cholera around the world. For example, Dr. Nathan Shaffer, an epidemiologist for the CDC, traveled to the small African nation of Guinea-Bissau in 1987 to help local doctors stop a massive outbreak

ROBERT KOCH EXPLAINS ANTHRAX

In the early 1870s, the German scientist Robert Koch finally proved what he and other scientists, such as Louis Pasteur, had long suspected—that germs cause disease. Koch hoped to show the connection between germs and disease by studying anthrax, a fatal disease of cattle, sheep, and other domesticated animals.

Koch had one important advantage over other researchers. One of the problems early microbiologists constantly encountered was that most germs did not live very long on a microscope slide. Without constant warmth, the germs died before scientists could observe a significant portion of their life cycles under magnification. Koch designed and built a special "warm-stage" microscope that allowed him to keep anthrax bacteria alive for much longer periods than had previously been possible. Thus, he could view almost the entire life cycle of these bacteria under his microscope.

Koch knew that periodic epidemics of anthrax wiped out herds of sheep and cattle throughout Europe. He suspected that germs infected and killed the animals, then entered the soil. Somehow, Koch reasoned, the germs managed to stay alive in the soil. Later, healthy animals became infected when they came into contact with the germs in the soil. Koch believed that this was why anthrax remained dormant, or inactive, before reappearing.

In his laboratory, Koch infected mice and other animals with the blood of sheep that had recently died of anthrax. He found that all of the animals injected contracted the disease, and also saw that the blood of all of the dead animals contained a certain kind of rod-shaped bacteria. Koch believed these were the bacteria that caused anthrax.

He placed some of the bacteria from the dead animals into his warm-stage microscope and watched them grow. After several hours the rods changed, forming a complex tangle of threads, which in turn were eventually transformed into tiny spores, or seed-like particles. Koch now needed to answer two questions. First, did these spores represent a reproductive stage of the anthrax bacteria? Second, could the spores infect healthy animals? If the spores did cause the animals to contract anthrax, it would mean that the spores transmitted the disease.

Koch injected some of the spores into laboratory mice and the animals soon came down with anthrax. He then observed the blood of the mice under his microscope. Instead of spores, the blood contained millions of rod-shaped bacteria identical to the ones that Koch had first observed. This proved that the spores were a reproductive stage of the bacteria that caused anthrax.

The cyclic way in which anthrax infected animals was now clear to Koch. Bacteria in diseased animals were transformed into spores, some of which entered the soil when the animals died. Tough and resistant to temperature extremes, the spores remained in the soil for months or years, until a healthy animal came along and ingested the spores by eating food grown in the contaminated soil.

Once in the animal's warm blood, the spores were transformed into the mature bacteria that caused anthrax, and the disease spread through its new host's body. In 1876, Koch presented his findings to German scientists at the University of Breslau. From there, the news traveled all over the world that Koch had established the connection between germs and disease.

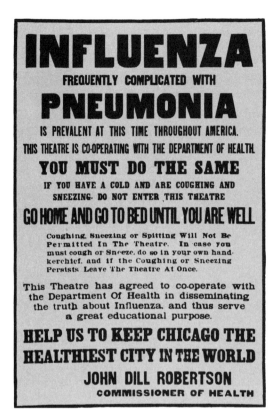

Among measures taken to prevent the spread of infectious disease in the late 19th and early 20th centuries were warnings, such as the public sign shown here, and quarantines, in which persons with certain diseases were legally restricted to their homes or institutions.

of cholera. His detective work began immediately. He had to figure out how the disease was infecting people on the seacoast and in the inland areas of the country. He knew that cholera often spreads through contaminated water, but the outbreaks did not seem to be associated with particular drinking-water wells.

Instead, the epidemic was spreading up and down the coast of Guinea-Bissau. Suspecting contamined shellfish as the cause of the epidemic, Shaffer realized that most of the people living along the coast ate a lot of shellfish, and also that contaminated shellfish tend to accumulate larger-than-normal amounts of cholera bacteria in their tissues. Shaffer went from house to house, asking people how and when they became ill, what they ate, and other questions pertinent to the epidemic. He also tested shellfish from local markets and found cholera bacteria, which explained how the people on the coast had contracted the disease. However, 80 people in an inland village had died from cholera, and when Shaffer traveled to the village, he found that none of the victims had eaten shellfish from the coast.

Shaffer searched for clues to this mystery. He learned that one of the villagers had been a dockworker on the coast who had recently died of cholera, and that his body had been shipped home. Shaffer then discovered that some of the same people who handled the body during the burial had also helped to prepare the funeral feast. Investigating further, Shaffer found that more than half the people who attended the feast had contracted cholera. A similar mystery was solved in 1978 by C. J. M. Rondle, an epidemiologist with the London School of Hygiene. He proposed a way in which people who lived in isolated areas, far from food and water contaminated with cholera, were catching the disease. Rondle observed that airliners often dumped solid wastes from their toilets into the atmosphere. Some of the bacteria in these infected wastes survived long enough to make it to the ground and spread the disease.

Disease detectives like Shaffer and Rondle realize that they must always be prepared to fight new outbreaks of such illnesses as cholera. Besides cholera, other diseases waiting to carry death abroad in the world include influenza, measles, typhoid fever, acquired immune deficiency syndrome (AIDS), hepatitis, tuberculosis, and many more. Epidemiologists and other doctors keep a close watch on these diseases, which threaten large numbers of people. They also monitor AIDS and other sexually transmitted diseases such as syphilis and gonorrhea, all of which will be discussed in chapter 5.

Other Methods of Disease Prevention

State and local boards of health also attempt to promote hygiene by preventing the spread of disease. These public organizations regularly inspect canning factories, restaurants, and other private businesses involved in the production and distribution of food. The improper handling, preparation, packaging, or cooking of various foods can all cause disease. Some diseases, such as salmonella infection and botulism, are associated with food poisoning. The problem of contaminated food, even in such modern wealthy countries as the United States and Britain, is greater than many people realize. From 20,000 to 30,000 cases of salmonella are reported in the United States each year, and experts estimate that this represents only about 10% of the actual total. Incidents of food poisoning can be serious. For example, in 1965, when contaminated turkey was accidentally served in a Syracuse University cafeteria, more than 50 students came down with severe stomach cramps and vomiting. Luckily, no one died.

Another way in which doctors and health officials work to prevent the spread of communicable diseases is through inoculations with vaccines, medicines developed to create immunity to specific diseases. Vaccines consist of a weakened or killed preparation of the disease-causing organism, such as a virus, which cannot produce a full-scale infection but which is sufficient to prompt the body's immune system

English physician Edward Jenner (1749–1823), shown here inoculating an infant, discovered vaccination as a means of preventing infectious disease. In the process of vaccination, a weakened or killed form of a virus or other disease-causing germ is introduced into the human body. This promotes the development of immunity to any future attack by the organism.

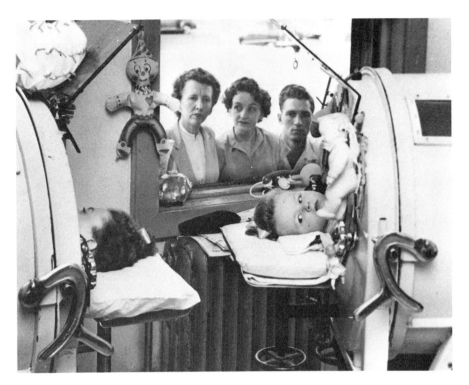

One disease against which vaccination has been highly successful is poliomyelitis. Before the widespread introduction of polio vaccine in the mid-1950s, poliomyelitis attacked tens of thousands of persons each year, crippling muscles in the limbs or respiratory system, often with fatal consequences. Persons in whom the disease attacked the muscles needed for breathing, such as these children in a U.S. hospital ward in 1952, were put into artificial respirators known as iron lungs, which enabled them to remain alive.

to recognize and destroy the fully active form of the organism should it ever enter the body. Unfortunately, an effective vaccine is not yet available for every disease, but thanks to the method of vaccination, some dread diseases that used to be widespread are now relatively rare. Among them are diphtheria; pertussis, or whooping cough; and tetanus, or lockjaw. Another is poliomyelitis, a potentially crippling disease that afflicted tens of thousands of Americans before the 1960s, killing many and paralyzing others for life.

German bacteriologist Robert Koch (1843–1910) proved Pasteur's germ theory of disease by showing that a specific kind of bacteria was responsible for spreading the disease known as anthrax among animals.

The advent of two kinds of vaccines—developed by Dr. Jonas Salk of the University of Pittsburgh and Dr. Albert Sabin of the University of Cincinnati—reduced the number of yearly cases of polio in the United States from an estimated 18,000 in 1954 to a mere 20 in 1978.

Education is also an important factor in limiting the spread of communicable diseases. Health officials have found that the more people are aware of the risks and consequences of these ailments, the easier it becomes to avoid serious epidemics. Almost all schools in industrialized countries now have health classes that stress the importance of good hygiene. These classes explain how communicable diseases spread and show people the best ways to avoid contracting these illnesses, including proper vaccination and inoculation, the correct preparation and cooking of food, drinking of purified water only, quarantining or separating the seriously ill from healthy persons, and seeing a doctor for physical symptoms that are out of the ordinary.

Magazine, radio, and television advertisements also stress some of these points. Unlike the situation in ages past, when the Black Death and other plagues regularly ravaged an ignorant populace, knowledge, science, and effective medicines today protect much of humanity from the threat of disease.

CHAPTER 3

PUBLIC HYGIENE PROGRAMS

The lack of widespread, adequate water-purification systems is a key factor in the continuing spread of disease in many underdeveloped countries. These Somalian women are washing clothes in water that is also used for drinking.

In many countries, public hygiene programs have proven essential to maintaining good health in large populations. Such programs include modern sewage treatment, garbage collection and recycling, control of insect pests, and the elimination of air and water pollution. All of these efforts help to promote better sanitation, reduce the spread of disease, and allow people to lead cleaner, healthier, and therefore safer lives.

Public hygiene programs began to be instituted on a widespread basis in the United States, Canada, and many European countries during the Industrial Revolution of the 1800s. In these developed countries, the introduction of new scientific methods and technologies in the 20th century made such components of sanitation as sewage treatment and pest control both more efficient and more effective. Today, scientists in these countries continue to develop new ways to improve public health.

Unfortunately, in many of the poorer countries of the world, sewage treatment and other sanitation programs are often inadequate or even nonexistent. In parts of Colombia, Bangladesh, and Ethiopia, for example, many people still drink from rivers and wells in which humans and animals regularly bathe and excrete their wastes. Sewage and garbage accumulates in streets, yards, and waterways, where it decays and breeds disease. Each year, millions of people in the poorer countries of the world die of disease and other problems associated with filth and poor sanitation.

An important goal of the United Nations Development Program, or UNDP, and the United Nations Population Fund, or UNPF, is to help impoverished countries to institute public hygiene programs. This goal is slowly being accomplished, partly with aid from wealthy, developed countries and partly through educational programs that teach the populations of less developed countries the importance of public hygiene facilities and practices. United Nations officials hope that public health systems, considered basic in developed countries, will be available everywhere in the world by the early 21st century.

Cleaning Water and Sewage

One of the public hygiene systems taken for granted in technologically advanced nations is water purification. Because these nations have widespread water purification systems, most of the diseases spread by drinking contaminated water—such as cholera, typhoid fever, and dysentery—are relatively rare. Most water purification plants use both filtration and chemical methods to clean water. In *filtration*, technicians force the water through layers of sand and gravel, with bacteria and

By contrast with the world's underdeveloped regions, modern nations have established widespread systems for water purification. Among the vital components of such systems are treatment plants, such as this one in New Orleans, Louisiana, that use chemical and other processes to render sewage harmless before passing it back into rivers or the ocean.

other impurities in the water being filtered out and collecting in the sand as the water passes through. Some of the most advanced filtration systems, which force the water through the sand under very high pressure, can purify as much as 150 million gallons of water per day.

In the chemical method of purifying water, technicians force chlorine gas through water. The chlorine gas immediately kills any germs that are present in the water. A dose of only one gallon of chlorine per 1 million gallons of water is more than enough to destroy the bacteria known as *Escherichia coli*, the most common type of germ found in contaminated water. Yet this dosage poses no threat to the people and animals who drink the water.

The treatment of sewage is another important public hygiene program. Sewage is the mixture of water and solid waste materials that humans routinely discard each day. It includes all of the human bodily wastes that are passed into toilets, as well as other wastes that enter into bathtubs, sinks, and street drains. The solid parts of sewage make up less than one-tenth of 1% of the total quantity of sewage, the rest being water. Yet in a large city, as much as 1,000 tons of these solid sewage materials, called sludge, can build up in a single day. Scientists and engineers regularly subject these wastes to chemical and other treatments in order to purify them before disposing of them.

While strong efforts are made to keep disease-causing germs out of the water supply, other germs play a valuable primary role in modern sewage treatment. These germs, normally present in water, soil, and other parts of the environment, feed on and digest sewage sludge, turning much of it into such harmless substances such as water, carbon dioxide, and various alcohols. Nearly all major cities in the United States now have sewage treatment facilities that use such germs on a large scale to purify wastes. Unfortunately, this is not the case in most

In order to be certain that it is free of disease-causing germs and other dangerous contaminants, water from reservoirs and other drinking sources must be tested regularly. The testing is done in laboratories such as the one shown here, whose sole purpose is to ascertain the purity of drinking water.

other countries of the world. For instance, more than 80% of the 125 largest cities located along the coasts of the Mediterranean Sea release untreated sewage directly into the sea.

The first step in modern sewage treatment, called *primary treatment*, separates the sludge from the liquid components of the sewage. The raw sewage is pumped into large open tanks, where the solid materials slowly settle to the bottom. During this process, germs begin to digest some of the sludge.

The next phase of the treatment process, called *secondary treatment*, is usually accomplished in two steps. In the first, the liquid portion of the sewage is aerated, or exposed to large amounts of air. The oxygen in the air encourages specific germs to grow quickly and digest particles of waste floating in the water. In the second step of secondary treatment, the solid wastes are pumped into special tanks, where other kinds of germs further digest and break down these wastes. One by-product created by this digestion is methane, a burnable gas. Many sewage treatment plants capture methane as it is released in the digestion of sewage, and use it as a fuel to help run the plants' machinery.

Scientists are constantly working to produce new strains of bacteria and other germs that will digest sewage more efficiently. One of the newest methods of sewage treatment is tertiary treatment, which uses a combination of germs and chemicals. Sewage treatment plants using this process attempt to purify liquid wastes so thoroughly that they can be recycled as drinking water. So far, this has been a costly process, but waste water treated in this manner is already being used to irrigate crops in many areas of the United States.

Buried in Trash

The question of what to do with garbage has become one of the greatest hygiene-related problems facing modern society. Most people are unaware of the tremendous amount of material regularly discarded in affluent countries such as the United States. At least 130 million tons of garbage are collected by garbage trucks alone in the United States each year, and the total yearly garbage buildup for the entire country

Despite the inconvenience and cost of water purification, industries and other sources continue to dump hundreds of millions of tons of raw waste materials into the waterways of the world's technologically advanced nations each year. This picture shows untreated wastes from an American meat-packing plant being discharged into a public waterway.

may exceed 250 million tons. This tremendous quantity of refuse poses a definite health threat. As writer Karen O'Connor points out,

"When we drop our trash on the street, toss it out a car window, or dump it into a lake or river, we pollute our cities, countryside, and waterways. . . . When we burn garbage in our backyard or at a city dump, we foul the air. When we leave it in the open, we spread disease. When we bury it, we risk having poisonous gases and liquids from the refuse seep into our drinking water." Such pollution hazards from open garbage dumps, referred to as sanitary landfills, prompted town officials to close half of the 10,500 garbage dumps in the United States between 1979 and 1989.

In recent years, two major efforts directed at dealing with the problem of garbage have begun in the United States and other developed countries. Together, these efforts may eventually end the practice of burying refuse in what are actually very unsanitary landfills. The first method involves building *transfer stations*, facilities to which people bring their garbage and throw it onto a conveyer belt. The belt loads the garbage into trucks, which transfer it to another location. In some cases, once the garbage is moved, it is simply buried as before, which only transfers the pollution and health threats from one town to another. However, many cities are now experimenting with compacting the garbage, treating it with special chemicals, and then burning it as a fuel for electrical and other utility companies and factories. In Baltimore, Maryland, for example, a special incinerator burns 2,250 tons of trash per day, generating heat for 500 city buildings and electricity for the Baltimore Gas & Electric Company. Thus, what was once useless refuse is routinely converted into very useful energy.

The other major effort to deal with garbage is *recycling*. Most towns and cities in the United States now have recycling centers, to which people can bring glass, plastic, metal, and paper refuse. The glass, for instance, is collected, melted down, and used to create new glass containers. From discarded newspapers and other paper products comes recycled paper not only for fresh newspapers and magazines but also for paper towels, toilet paper, napkins, and greeting cards. Recycling and other modern methods of dealing with refuse reduce the health threat posed by garbage while at the same time helping to maintain a cleaner, more attractive environment.

When the Air Is Unfit To Breathe

In addition to the health threat from garbage, the public must contend with another environmental threat—air pollution. There are several kinds of air pollution, all damaging to health. Perhaps the most serious kind of air pollution that now faces society, however, is smog.

Smog, a phenomenon associated with factories and large numbers of cars and trucks, dirties the air over cities and countrysides alike. The word *smog*, a combination of the words *smoke* and *fog*, originally described the thick brown haze that hung over many industrial cities beginning in the 19th century. This haze was composed of familiar primary pollutants, such as carbon dioxide, sulfur dioxide, and soot. The health danger posed by smog was amply illustrated in 1948 in the steel mill town of Donora, Pennsylvania.

In Donora, weather conditions allowed smog from the mills to build up into a lethal cloud that choked the air, killing 17 people and hospitalizing hundreds of others. In the early 20th century, Pittsburgh, Pennsylvania—also the site of steel mills as well as other factories—

earned the nickname Smoke City because of its frequent onsets of industrial smog.

By contrast, most modern smog forms when combinations of primary pollutants from car and truck exhausts react with sunlight to produce thick concentrations of *ozone*, a gas similar to, but heavier than, oxygen. Scientists usually refer to ozone smog as *photochemical smog*. The city that has suffered the most from photochemical smog is Los Angeles, California. In the late 1930s, the city began to expand, and by the early 1960s, there were more motor vehicles in southern California than in any other area of comparable size in the United States. This gave Los Angeles one of the factors needed for the creation of a severe ozone smog—plenty of primary pollutants. Unfortunately, the city already had two other factors that promote smog—its location in a flat basin surrounded by mountains, and exposure to plenty of sunlight. All three of these factors combined to produce huge quantities of ozone and serious photochemical smog, and a thick haze sometimes hid the tallest buildings in the city from view. By the mid-1960s, Los Angeles city officials often issued ozone alerts, advising children and elderly persons to stay indoors. To prevent the ozone that blanketed the city from being widely and deeply inhaled, the officials warned everyone not to exert themselves.

Eventually, Los Angles managed to reduce its low-level ozone concentrations, partly because laws and devices to reduce air pollution, instituted in the 1970s, eliminated many of the pollutants released by cars and other vehicles. Nevertheless, although ozone alerts now happen only infrequently in Los Angeles, ozone levels in the city remain high. Los Angeles is not the only city facing this problem. During the summer of 1988, for example, some 96 cities and counties in the United States repeatedly registered smog levels considered dangerous to public health. And the problem is even worse in many foreign countries. Photochemical smog laced with ozone hangs over dozens of cities from Athens, Greece, to Tokyo, Japan.

Efforts in the United States to reduce the health threat of smog began in the 1970s when the U.S. Environmental Protection Agency (EPA) demanded that cars, trucks, and factories emit fewer pollutants. By law, all cars were required to have catalytic converters—devices that filter out many of the worst pollutants from automobile exhausts. Although the EPA's efforts were helpful, they made only a small dent in the smog problem. In 1990, President George Bush signed a new Clean Air Act with the goal of ending the smog problem by the year 2000. Some of the act's proposals include using more effective filters on factory smokestacks and building more cars that run on alcohol and electricity, which produce fewer pollutants. Whether these efforts will eliminate the problem of smog remains to be seen.

Battling Dangerous Pests

Another area of concern to public health is pest control. In developed countries, rodent pests, such as rats, are not a widespread problem. Instead, health authorities direct most of their money and energies to battling insect pests, many of which carry dangerous disease germs or cause serious damage to crops. In their quest for new ways to eliminate

Smog caused by automobile exhaust, factory smoke, and other wastes remains a serious source of respiratory and other diseases in the world's industrialized regions. The density that smog can achieve—often unrecognized at ground level—is shown in this aerial photograph of Denver, Colorado.

An experimental weapon in the battle against smog is the electric automobile, one version of which is shown here. Because they run entirely on electricity, such vehicles produce no smog-creating exhaust.

insect pests, scientists in the 20th century have developed insecticides, substances that kill insects. Although such chemical insecticides as DDT—an abbreviation for the chemical name dichloro-diphenyl-tri-chloro-ethane—effectively kill insects, insecticides are not broken down by germs living in the soil or by natural processes, which means that the insecticides often remain in the soil as toxic pollutants, eventually getting into the water supply and poisoning fish and other food sources used by animals and humans.

One of the most promising new methods for destroying insect pests without causing environmental pollution is to use bacteria that infect and kill insects. The German scientist G. S. Berliner first proposed this idea in the early 1900s. Berliner noticed that certain kinds of bacteria destroyed moth caterpillars. But the way in which the bacteria did this was not well understood at the time, and the idea was largely forgotten until the 1970s and 1980s.

Scientists eventually learned that while they are reproducing, the bacteria that Berliner had observed produce highly toxic poisons. These poisons accumulate on plant leaves and are ingested by the caterpillars of moths, butterflies, and related insects when they eat the leaves. Once inside the caterpillar's digestive tract, or gut, the poisons dissolve the gut walls, and the insect soon becomes paralyzed and dies.

To make the bacterial insecticide, scientists grow large cultures of the bacteria and harvest them at the time when they are producing the toxic poison. The bacteria are then dried and made into a dusting powder that can be sprinkled on crops by ground-based machines or airplanes. This method is now regularly used to control such pests as tomato hornworms, gypsy moth caterpillars, alfalfa caterpillars, and cabbageworms.

Insecticides and other pest-killing substances, widely used to protect crops of food plants, have also assumed important roles in preventing human disease. One insect against which such substances have been directed is the deer tick, which spends part of its life cycle on deer and is the cause of the human infection known as Lyme disease.

An important advantage of bacterial insecticides is that they appear to be harmless to plants and other animals. The poisons break down quickly into nontoxic substances that do not accumulate in the soil, making the method environmentally safe. Farmers have reported such a high rate of success with this approach to pest control that scientists are experimenting with bacteria that might be used to kill other kinds of insect pests, especially those that carry deadly diseases.

Public health programs that provide clean water, deal with sewage and garbage, work to eliminate air pollution, and fight insect pests are among the most important tools for promoting good hygiene in modern society. These programs are often expensive, but they represent some of the best examples of public tax money being spent for the good of everyone. Without these large-scale hygienic efforts, which so many people tend to take for granted, the United States and other affluent countries would quickly return to the world of disease, famine, and misery of ages past.

CHAPTER 4

HYGIENE IN THE HOME

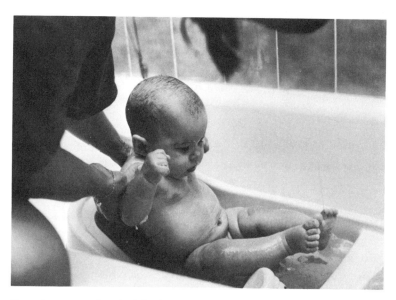

Regular grooming habits, including bathing, washing one's hair, and brushing one's teeth are necessary for cleansing the body of potentially harmful germs that reside on the skin and hair, as well as in the mouth. For maximum benefit, such habits should be taught at an early stage in life, as in the case of the infant shown here.

The same hygienic principles that guide local authorities in safeguarding the health of the community also apply to individual homes. Home hygiene includes every factor in a house or apartment that affects the health and safety of the persons living there, including habits of personal cleanliness, refuse and garbage disposal, proper heating, lighting, and ventilation, and the prevention of accidents.

According to hygiene expert Dr. John Gibson, "One of the best ways of keeping healthy is to live in a house [that is] dry, warm and in a state of good repair. It should have drinking water available inside . . . and adequate facilities for heating water; satisfactory places for storing, preparing and cooking food; sinks, a bath[tub] and a . . . [toilet]; an adequate drainage system; adequate lighting, natural and artificial; adequate ventilation and facilities for heating each room."

Most people in affluent countries take these things for granted. Yet in many developing countries, and even in certain parts of the United States, inadequate plumbing, heating, and other housing factors contribute to above-normal rates of disease and accidental injury. And in homes where these facilities are lacking, it is often difficult to develop and practice personally hygienic grooming habits.

Developing a Sense of Personal Hygiene

The importance of personal cleanliness is twofold. First, it reduces the risk of catching and spreading infectious diseases and parasites. Millions of bacteria inhabit both the inside and outside of every person's body at any given moment. This is perfectly normal and nothing to worry about, because the vast majority of these germs are quite harmless. In fact, some of the bacteria that live inside the human body cannot live anywhere else, and actually aid in such bodily processes as digestion.

By contrast, some other germs that live on or in the body are not so harmless. For example, certain types of bacteria multiply rapidly in the mouth, causing tooth decay and gum disease. And people are sometimes exposed to other, more harmful germs, as well as to such insect parasites as body lice and ticks, which also make their homes on the body. Regular grooming habits, such as bathing, washing one's hair, and brushing one's teeth, help keep these unwanted pests from multiplying and adversely affecting a person's health. Brushing one's teeth after a meal, for example, protects the teeth and gums by eliminating food particles, on which decay-causing bacteria thrive.

Personal cleanliness is also important for social reasons. Most people are made uncomfortable or even repulsed by someone who regularly displays poor grooming habits. This is very different from the situation in many past cultures, such as medieval Europe, in which

In addition to bathing, hair washing, and toothbrushing, good grooming includes maintaining a neat appearance—a skill that this little girl has already learned.

regular bathing and grooming were the exception rather than the rule. Perhaps attitudes about personal hygiene have changed because humans have learned so much in the past century and a half about the causes and spread of disease; today, many people probably dislike uncleanliness because they tend to associate it with disease.

Persons who rarely bathe, wash their hair, or brush their teeth also tend to look slovenly and have body odors and bad breath that are considered socially unacceptable. No set rules govern the frequency of personal grooming. However, assuming that one has adequate plumbing facilities, a bath or shower once a day is a commonsense approach to cleanliness from the standpoint of both health and social acceptability. Showering after strenuous work or exercise is also a practical measure. Regular washing of the hands is another important habit, because people constantly touch their mouths, noses, ears, food, objects in public places, and toilet facilities with their bare hands. This is why it is so important to wash one's hands after using the toilet, after changing babies, and especially before preparing food. In order to prevent tooth decay, teeth should be flossed once a day, and dentists recommend brushing the teeth after every meal.

Food Storage and Disposal

Among the most important aspects of hygiene in the home are the proper handling, storage, and preparation of food. Because food can easily spoil or become contaminated with germs, improper handling of food often leads to health problems. Bacteria from the air, utensils, or hands often enter food containers, where they rapidly multiply, doubling their numbers every 15 minutes at room temperature. This is why few foods exposed to the air keep well at room temperature.

Both very cold and very hot temperatures help to protect food from contamination. Because cold slows the growth of bacteria, storing foods in a refrigerator keeps them edible for a longer period than they

Regular dental examinations are also an important part of good hygiene. They enable the dentist to detect and treat tooth decay and other diseases of the teeth and gums at an early stage, before such diseases cause serious damage.

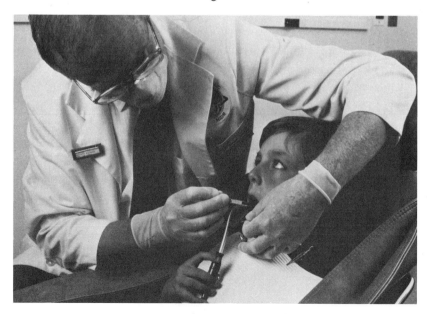

would keep at room temperature, although they will still spoil if stored long enough. Thus, most leftovers, even when refrigerated, should be eaten within a week.

Freezing foods keeps them much longer than refrigerating them, but even this does not preserve them indefinitely, and it is best to consume most frozen foods within a few months to a year after freezing them. It is also important to keep frozen foods tightly wrapped and to check them periodically to see that they have not become freezer burned. Information about how long different foods can be safely kept frozen is available from the National Agricultural Library in Beltsville, Maryland. Heating foods destroys germs rather than slowing their growth, as does freezing. Cooking most foods at temperatures above 150° Fahrenheit will kill most of the bacteria that might adversely affect the health of persons eating the food.

The means used to dispose of leftover or unwanted food in the home can also affect a family's health. Once food is discarded at room temperature, germs immediately begin to multiply in it. Also, flies seek out the waste food and lay eggs in it, rapidly producing maggots that thrive on decaying food. Besides this, the odor of rotting food attracts animals looking for a free meal. Thus, garbage that contains food should be disposed of quickly, ideally by taking it to the nearest landfill or refuse-treatment facility. If garbage must be kept around the house or garage for more than a day, it should be tightly wrapped in plastic bags and stored in a metal garbage can equipped with a lid. Garbage of any kind should be kept well away from food storage and preparation areas.

Pets and Pests

The rat is one of the animals most often attracted to rotting garbage. The types of rats that most commonly infest human habitations are the brown rat and the black rat. As John Gibson explains in his book *Health: Personal and Communal*, "Rats do an enormous amount of damage. They eat grain, root crops, fruit and vegetables. They kill and eat poultry and game. They destroy woodwork, strip insulating materials off electric wires, perforate pipes, and tear up clothing for nesting material." Most importantly from a health standpoint, rats carry and spread disease. Mice are less destructive than rats but also contaminate food with disease-causing germs. The best way to prevent these rodents from entering and infesting a house is to keep all foods covered and stored either in the refrigerator or in secure cupboards. Also, as mentioned earlier, keeping garbage around, especially when it is left uncovered and unprotected, is an open invitation to rodents. A clean home where food is properly stored and disposed of will not attract rodents. If a house appears to be infested with mice or rats, the best course is to call a professional exterminator, who knows how to safely dispose of rodents. Homeowners who attempt to kill these animals with various poisons run the risk of exposing children or pets to these poisons.

The most common insect pests in the home are cockroaches, ants, and flies. Cockroaches and ants are not known to carry disease, but can foul food with their waste materials. Cockroaches live in cracks in floors, under appliances, and inside walls, most often near food supplies, and they breed quickly. Ants do not usually nest in homes, but rather crawl in from outside looking for food. When ants do make a nest inside a house, however, the colony will contain thousands of members and must be eliminated by a professional. In eliminating insect pests, the same word of caution applies as in eliminating rodents.

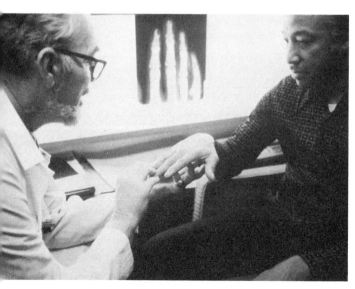

An important component of good hygiene is a regular medical checkup by a physician. Such checkups reveal hidden illnesses when they exist and are reassuring when they find nothing abnormal.

A professional exterminator is the best judge of how to rid a home of various insects in a safe and reliable manner.

Flies also spread serious diseases, including diarrhea, dysentery, and worm infections. They do this by crawling on and laying eggs in animal wastes and rotting garbage, then landing on exposed food on kitchen counters and elsewhere. Disease germs or the eggs of parasitic worms fall from the flies' mouths or legs and contaminate the food. Once again, keeping food covered and protected before preparing it, as well as properly disposing of garbage, usually eliminates this problem.

Rodents and insects are not the only animals that can cause hygiene problems in the home. Though most people do not realize it, pets can carry harmful diseases and transmit some of them to humans. Thus, for example, both dogs and cats commonly carry *Salmonella* bacteria, which may or may not make the animals sick. This bacteria can cause the serious human disease typhoid fever, as well as various other infectious diseases. Health authorities estimate that as many as 20% of all dogs and cats in the United States carry this disease at any given time. Humans can contract salmonella poisoning by directly handling these animals or by contact with dust contaminated by the animals' fecal matter. Dogs and cats can also spread multicellular parasites such as roundworms to humans. The best way to ensure the health of both pets and humans in a household is to have a veterinarian inspect the animals on a regular basis, so that treatment can be immediately prescribed for worms or other problems. Also, keeping pets away from human food and washing one's hands after handling an animal help to prevent potential pet-related health problems.

Physical Aspects of the Home

Spoiled food and animal pests, which can spread infectious diseases, are among the most obvious health-related factors in the average home. Nevertheless, a number of other factors, although much less obvious, are just as important to the health of family members. These include proper heating, lighting, and ventilation, as well as the safety of the materials used in constructing the family's house.

Home heating systems should support good health, not only by providing warmth, but also by operating in a safe manner. Heating systems that produce smoke or noxious fumes, that can scald or burn people, or that pose a high risk of fires or explosions should obviously be avoided, and most such heating systems are fortunately things of the past. Most modern home heating systems in developed countries like the United States utilize one of three basic types of energy: oil, natural gas, or electricity. Each type of system has its advantages and disadvantages, and all are relatively safe as long as they function normally. It is important to have a home furnace or other heating system inspected on a yearly basis to make sure it is running safely and efficiently. A defective or aging system can cause a disastrous fire.

The need for ventilation is tied directly to the type of heating system in a home; clean-burning heating systems, for example, do not pollute the air in the home. Besides being clean, however, the air inside the home must circulate and be regularly replenished with fresh air from outside. Poor ventilation can make people sleepy and faint, and can lead to loss of appetite and other physical problems. In most homes, ventilation is not a major problem; in summer the windows can be opened and in winter the temperature difference between the inside and outside of the home forces an exchange of air through chimneys and cracks around doors and windows. Homes that are unusually airtight and in which windows are kept shut for long periods should have an electric fan built into an outside wall to ensure that air circulates inside the home.

Poor lighting is a health hazard because it can adversely affect vision. Many people read or do other detailed visual work under lighting that is too dim, which puts a strain on the eyes. Reading lights should be bright and should shine directly on the material that is being read. Lights placed across the room or behind the reader are not adequate for this. Another lighting problem is glare from lights that are too bright, a situation that strains the eyes in a different way and causes drowsiness. A bare light bulb should not shine directly into the eyes, even when one is not looking directly at the bulb. Instead, the light should always be shaded. Also, care should be taken not to allow lights to create reflections on television screens, because this also strains the eyes.

The two most common building materials that have proven to be health hazards in homes, schools, and offices are lead paint and asbestos. Before the 1960s, almost all paints contained lead. Then, doctors and scientists proved that thousands of children in the United States and other countries were suffering from lead poisoning caused by their having accidentally consumed lead-based paints. Because lead poisoning can cause brain damage and other problems, paint manufacturers no longer use lead in their products, and much of the lead paint on old buildings has been removed. Nevertheless, a great deal of lead paint remains, and many new cases of paint-related lead poisoning are reported each year. Anyone who suspects that the paint in his or her home contains lead should have a professional test a sample of the paint and, if necessary, remove any lead paint.

Asbestos is an extremely fire-resistant mineral that was once used extensively in the construction of homes, schools, and other buildings. However, researchers eventually discovered that particles of asbestos routinely become dislodged and travel through the air, where some of them are inhaled into people's lungs. These particles can irritate the tissues of the lungs, as well as causing pneumonialike symptoms and even lung cancer. Like lead paint, asbestos is now being removed from many structures, especially schools. Sometimes, it is not possible to remove all of the asbestos from a building, in which case a professional can suggest ways of containing the asbestos and keeping its particles from circulating in the air.

Special care must be taken to safeguard children against accidental poisoning and other injuries caused by cleaning materials, medicines, and other chemical substances used in the home. The best way to do this is to keep such materials in a locked cabinet or other space that children cannot reach or open.

Avoiding Home Accidents

The most common types of accidents are those that occur in the home, making such accidents an important concern in human health. The magnitude of the problem is much greater than most people realize. For instance, in Great Britain, with a population of about 58 million, some 10,000 people die in home accidents each year, and another 100,000 are hospitalized. In the United States, home accidents killed more than 20,000 persons in 1991 and were responsible for more than 20 million injuries from 1985 to 1987. Some of the most common accidents are falls, burns, chokings, and poisonings. Health authorities claim that most of these accidents are preventable. For example, objects left on stairs are among the leading causes of falls. If family members are careful about never leaving anything on the stairs, this type of fall becomes very unlikely. Another common home accident—fire caused by the overloading of an electrical outlet or extension cord—is also easily preventable if everyone in the family is taught never to plug more than one major electrical device, such as a toaster or space heater, into a single outlet or cord at one time.

Special care must be taken to safeguard children, particularly infants and toddlers, from home accidents. This means making sure that cabinets containing medicines, cleaning products, and other potentially dangerous materials are locked away or otherwise secured or are located beyond the reach of children, that electrical sockets are fitted with child-proof safety plugs, and that small children are not allowed near hot stove burners or hot water faucets. It is equally important to prevent young children from falling out of windows, by installing protective devices on the windows, and protecting children from head injuries caused by falling on sharp corners or hard objects. In general, proper supervision of children by their parents or older siblings will prevent most serious home accidents. Like other health-related factors in the home, such as the sanitary handling of food and the proper care of pets, avoiding accidents is largely a matter of being careful and conscientious.

CHAPTER 5

SEXUAL HYGIENE

A rack of contraceptive devices in a pharmacy. In addition to preventing unwanted pregnancies, the use of such devices has become vital in preventing the spread of sexually transmitted diseases.

Sexual hygiene may be defined as the practices and precautions that keep the genital organs clean and free of disease, and that prevent the spread of sexually transmitted disease. Until recently, most older members of society, including parents, educators, publishers, and even some doctors, were reluctant to discuss issues relating to sexual hygiene. This stemmed from long-standing customs, including the idea that it was socially unacceptable to talk openly about such a private matter as sexuality. Moreover, many parents and other older persons feared that the more young people knew about sex, the more likely they would be to engage in sex. One such belief, which continues to exist among large numbers of people, is that detailed knowledge about *contraceptives*—the devices used during sexual intercourse to prevent pregnancy—would lead young people into promiscuity, or frequent, indiscriminate sexual behavior. This, it was feared, would in turn lead to increasing numbers of unwanted pregnancies.

Within the past two decades, these fears have been largely put to rest. Teaching young people the facts about sex and the risks involved in sexual intercourse has been proven to promote more responsible sexual behavior, rather than less responsibility. Studies have shown that those persons who are best educated about sex are the least likely to engage in it indiscriminately, have unwanted pregnancies, or contract sexually transmitted diseases.

Beginning in the 1960s and 1970s, such topics as sexual practices, contraception, and sexually transmitted diseases increasingly became the subjects of magazine and newspaper articles, television talk shows, and even school textbooks. In the 1980s, these topics frequently became front-page news because of the discovery that the virus that causes AIDS, which can be transmitted through intimate sexual contact, was spreading rapidly within the American population. As AIDS began to reach epidemic proportions in the late 1980s, it became clear that the public urgently needed specific and frank information about how to avoid contracting the disease. Once again, doctors, health authorities, and educators learned that the most effective way to combat AIDS and other sexually transmitted diseases is to educate people about these illnesses and the risks involved in various kinds of sexual contact.

Cleaning of the Genital Areas

Before considering the risk of acquiring a sexually transmitted disease, it is important to emphasize the need to regularly clean the genital area—advice that applies to both men and women. Over the course of several days, perspiration, natural secretions, and traces of urine can collect in or around the genitals. Because the genitals are warm and moist, these collections can become breeding grounds for bacteria that cause local infections of the urinary tract. These infections are often characterized by irritation or pain on urination; yellow, white, or clear discharges; and occasionally by swelling around the genitals. Although such infections are not usually serious, they are uncomfortable, and because they can sometimes be passed from one person to another through sexual contact, they should be prevented or brought to the attention of a doctor if they do occur.

Daily bathing greatly reduces the risk of these infections. Men who are uncircumcised should take special care to wash under the foreskin of the penis, where infections are most likely to occur. Similarly, women should make sure that the areas around the labia, the folds of skin surrounding the vagina, are kept clean. According to doctors, it is unnecessary to douche, or clean the inside of the vagina, on a regular basis. They advise women who insist upon douching to do so infrequently and to use only a mixture of water and vinegar. Too frequent douching can disrupt the balance of beneficial bacteria normally present in the vagina and thus increase the chance of infection.

Another aspect of genital hygiene that specifically affects women is dealing with their menstrual periods. Beginning when girls reach puberty, menstruation occurs about once a month in females who are not pregnant. In menstruation, cells that make up the lining of the uterus are discharged through the vagina, along with blood that oozes from the lining of the uterus when it sheds these cells. Women need to be especially careful about keeping the genital area clean during menstruation. Tampons inserted into the vagina to absorb the menstrual flow of blood and uterine cells should be changed at least every four to six hours, even if they have absorbed little or no material. Tampons left in place for too long a time carry an increased risk of producing toxic shock syndrome, a serious bacterial infection that can be fatal. As is the case at other times of the month, it is also unnecessary to douche during menstruation.

What Are STDs?

Although it is important to keep the genital area clean, this does not decrease the risk of acquiring a *sexually transmitted disease*, or STD. Such diseases, which used to be called venereal diseases, after Venus, the Roman goddess of love, are spread from one person to another almost exclusively by intimate sexual activity, including vaginal and anal intercourse and oral sex. A mother infected with an STD may also pass it along to the fetus while it is in her womb or during childbirth.

STDs are serious diseases that cause discomfort or pain and, if not treated, can damage the sexual and reproductive organs as well as other tissues and organs of the body. Some are potentially fatal. Fortunately, most STDs can be cured with proper treatment, which is why all persons should be aware of the symptoms of these diseases and should immediately consult a doctor upon detecting any such symptom.

Unfortunately, some people who develop an STD are too embarrassed to mention it. Much of this embarrassment is due to the social stigma, or disgrace, that once surrounded these diseases, and to a population that believed only sinful or promiscuous people contracted STDs. Today that attitude has largely disappeared; educated persons know that germs do not discriminate, and that acquiring an STD has nothing to do with one's social status, sexual preference, race, or frequency of sexual activity. The truth is that anyone can get an STD and pass it on to a sexual partner. Thus, someone who contracts an STD should feel no shame in seeking prompt treatment for it, much as someone would seek treatment for a severe case of influenza.

Different Types of STDs

Humans can acquire many different kinds of STDs. Some are caused by bacteria and others by viruses. Some are relatively easy to treat, while others, such as AIDS, which will be discussed later, are very difficult to treat. All STDs should be taken seriously. One of the most common STDs is *gonorrhea*, sometimes referred to as the clap or the drip. The symptoms of this bacterial infection usually appear 2 to 22 days after a person is infected. In women, symptoms of gonorrhea include a thick yellow or white discharge from the vagina, a burning sensation during urination, and cramps in the lower abdomen. Symptoms experienced by men are a thick yellow or white discharge from the penis and a burning sensation during urination or bowel movements. It is important to stress that in some cases, men or women who have gonorrhea do not exhibit these symptoms, and the disease can go undetected for a long time. This is one reason why everyone should have regular medical checkups. Left untreated, gonorrhea can damage the reproductive organs and lead to heart trouble and skin disease. By contrast, gonorrhea is easily cured if detected early and properly treated with antibiotics.

The symptoms of chlamydial infection and nongonococcal urethritis, or NGU, are largely similar to those of gonorrhea. One difference is that women with chlamydia sometimes experience mild bleeding from the vagina between their regular menstrual periods. As with gonorrhea, many people with NGU or chlamydial infection do not experience any of the normal symptoms. Like gonorrhea, chlamydia and NGU left untreated can cause damage to the reproductive organs, making it impossible for a man or a woman who has the disease to have children. Also like gonorrhea, both chlamydia and NGU are easy to treat successfully if detected early.

Herpes is an STD caused by a virus. The symptoms of herpes generally show up 2 to 30 days after having sex, and include flulike feelings, itching or burning sensations around the mouth or genital areas, and small sores or blisters in these same areas. The herpes sores usually last from one to three weeks and then disappear temporarily. This does not mean that the disease has gone away, but rather that it has "gone underground," or ceased to show external symptoms. The sores reappear periodically, at which times the disease is extremely infectious. At present, there is no cure for herpes.

Genital warts, or condylomata, also caused by a virus, are growths that develop on the sexual organs or anus, or both, and do not go away. Because they are accompanied by itching or burning sensations, these warts can be very uncomfortable. They are also unsightly, often causing considerable embarrassment to the infected person. The longer genital warts go untreated, the more of them grow and the harder they are to

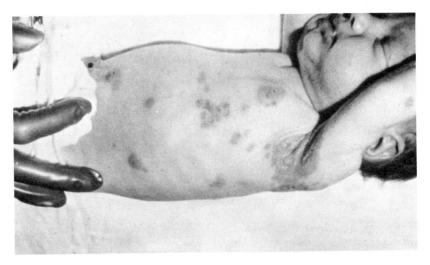

An infant infected with herpesvirus, which it acquired from its in-fected mother before it was born. Herpesvirus infections of this type are among several sexually transmitted diseases that mothers can pass along to their offspring before or during birth.

get rid of. Among treatments for eliminating genital warts are freezing, burning them off with electricity or lasers, and removing them by surgery.

Although syphilis is a relatively rare disease, it is one of the most serious of the STDs, and an increasing number of cases have recently been reported. Left untreated, syphilis can lead to heart disease, brain damage, blindness, and eventually death. The symptoms appear in two stages. In the first stage, 1 to 12 weeks after a person is infected, a painless sore appears on the mouth or sexual organs. The sore goes away after a few weeks, but this only means that the disease has gone underground. In the second stage, six weeks to six months after the appearance of the sore, a rash and flulike symptoms may appear. These also disappear, but the disease continues to progressively damage the internal organs. Syphilis can be detected by a blood test.

Protecting Against STDs

According to doctors and health authorities, several precautions can and should be taken by everyone to help prevent the spread of STDs. First, a person should be careful about his or her sexual partners. Before having sex, one should look on the partner for signs of sores, rashes, warts, or discharges. If any of these signs are present, sex should be avoided until the partner sees a doctor and receives treatment. One should also ask a potential sexual partner if he or she has ever had an STD. This may seem like an embarrassing thing to do, but most people would agree that it is preferable to contracting an STD. Very importantly, persons who are not *monogamous* (with one partner exclusively for a long time), should use some kind of protection. The most effective protection is a condom, or rubber, which should be used for oral and anal sex as well as for vaginal intercourse. Birth-control foams, creams, and jellies will kill most, although not all, STD germs.

Knowing and always watching for the symptoms of STDs are very important in preventing the spread of these diseases. People who are not monogamous, and especially those who have several sexual partners within a six-month or one-year period, should have a doctor check for STDs at least every six months. Also—and very important— is that anyone diagnosed with an STD should immediately inform all of his or her sexual partners so that they can receive treatment and halt further spread of the disease.

The Threat of AIDS

AIDS is the newest and potentially the most threatening of the STDs. The facts that have come to light since doctors first learned about the disease illustrate how ignorance and misconceptions can allow STDs to reach epidemic proportions. The first reported cases of the AIDs occurred in 1981, all involving young homosexual, or gay, men. Something was causing the victims' immune systems to become impaired, allowing them to contract pneumonia and a rare form of cancer. In the following months, the CDC in Atlanta received more than 500 reports of such cases from around the United States, all involving gay men who had strange deficiencies of the immune system.

CDC laboratories tested samples of the victims' blood, urine, feces, and saliva, but found no unusual germs. Yet something was clearly attacking and destroying the victims' immune systems, leaving their bodies open to infection. Was the disease being spread through sexual contact? This seemed a strong possibility, considering that most of the victims reported having a number of sexual partners.

By early 1982, similar cases began to be seen among drug users who shared needles and people who had received blood transfusions. These victims were both male and female, and most were not gay. The medical investigators now had reason to believe that the new disease spread through contact with infected blood, during sexual activity, drug use, or blood transfusion. The illness was not a disease of homosexuals, as some people had thought. The gay community had simply been the first group in the United States to be ravaged by the disease. In the summer of 1982, doctors began to call the illness acquired immune deficiency syndrome, or AIDS. As hundreds of new cases were reported in the United States and many other countries, the race was on to find the cause.

In 1983 and 1984, doctors in the United States and France isolated a virus called HTLV-3 and identified it as the cause of AIDS. Appar-

A microscopic view of Treponema pallidum, *the parasitic organism that causes syphilis. Although no longer as common as it once was, syphilis is nevertheless among the most serious sexually transmitted diseases, with the ability to damage the heart, brain, and eyes and eventually to cause death.*

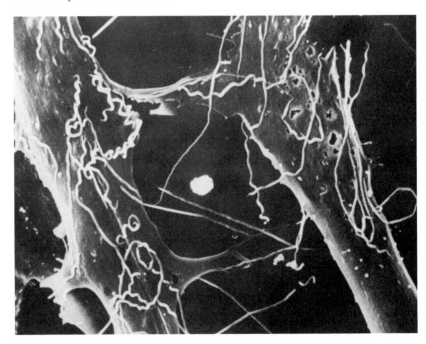

Earvin "Magic" Johnson of the Los Angeles Lakers, one of the most outstanding players in the history of basketball, announced on November 7, 1991, that he was retiring from the game because he had become infected with the human immunodeficiency virus that causes AIDS.

ently, the virus attacks T cells, the white blood cells that form a major line of defense in the immune system. The AIDS virus multiplies in the cells, eventually destroying them and crippling the immune system. An international committee of scientists later renamed the virus HIV, which stands for human immunodeficiency virus. Late in 1984, Dr. Robert Gallo, of the NIH, found a way to produce large quantities of the HIV virus for study. This allowed doctors to develop a laboratory test that detects the virus in the blood of those infected with it.

Although there is still no cure for AIDS, it is now possible for doctors to diagnose the disease with relatively high accuracy. Physicians know that in addition to leaving the body open to other diseases, HIV can cause symptoms of its own in some people. These symptoms can include extreme fatigue, swollen glands in the neck and armpits, unusual weight loss, a long-lasting heavy cough, continuous bouts of diarrhea, and bruises that form easily and last a long time. Such symptoms, as well as the occurrence of unusually severe infections or immune-system problems, alert doctors to the possible presence of AIDS. But the fact that doctors can diagnose AIDS has not checked the spread of the disease. All through the 1980s, most heterosexuals did not take the threat of AIDS seriously. Assuming that only gay people and drug addicts were at risk, many heterosexuals continued to have unprotected sex. By the late 1980s, it became clear that the spread of AIDS through heterosexual contact was quickly increasing. By 1991, medical authorities estimated that millions of people in the United States and perhaps tens of millions around the world were carrying the AIDS virus.

The fact that anyone can contract AIDS received widespread attention in November 1991, when world famous basketball star Earvin "Magic" Johnson announced that he had to quit the game because he had HIV. In a courageous speech, Johnson made it clear that he had become infected with the virus through heterosexual sex and promised to help in the campaign to educate the public about it. In accordance with the available medical evidence, Johnson advised people to limit the number of their sexual partners, to wear condoms during all sexual activity, and to get regular medical checkups. Johnson's message is important because this kind of cautious and responsible behavior could slow the spread of all STDs and help bring about a healthier society.

CHAPTER 6

PREVENTING NON-COMMUNICABLE DISEASES

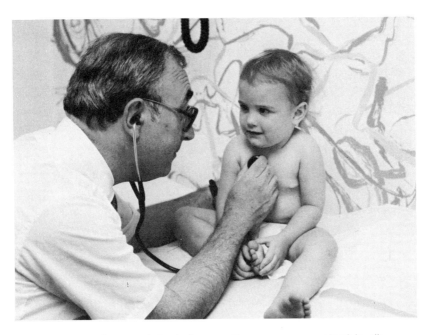

A doctor examines an infant. Among the noncommunicable diseases that begin early in life is heart disease. Although it ordinarily produces no visible effects for many years, heart disease often begins before the age of 20, when a fatty substance known as cholesterol forms deposits in blood vessels of the heart and other organs. Later in life, these deposits become large enough to obstruct the vessels, causing heart attacks.

One very important part of everyone's personal approach to hygiene should be developing and maintaining habits that decrease the risk of noncommunicable diseases. Unlike *communicable diseases*, which are caused and spread by germs, *noncommunicable diseases* are illnesses that cannot be passed from one person to another.

Examples are cancer, emphysema, heart disease, and diabetes. The occurrence of noncommunicable diseases is influenced by various factors, including heredity, diet, exercise, exposure to radiation as well as harmful chemicals, stress, and the use of drugs. Sometimes, two or more factors contribute to a single disease. A diet containing substantial quantities of fat and cholesterol, for example, can lead to heart and artery disease. For someone who consumes such a diet and who also smokes and is frequently under stress, the risk of heart disease is greatly increased. But unlike heredity, over which no one has any control, such factors as diet and smoking are readily controllable. Any habits or behaviors that tend to increase the risks of noncommunicable diseases are detrimental to health and should therefore be reduced or eliminated.

Cancer and Emphysema

Cancer is one of the most widespread and dangerous of the noncommunicable diseases. The general term *cancer* refers to several related diseases in which body cells grow and spread in an abnormal way. In his book *Dimensions: A Changing Concept of Health*, health expert Kenneth Jones points out that throughout life, the cells in many parts of the body are constantly dividing to provide replacements for worn out or damaged cells, but that in cancer, the normal, orderly division and growth of these cells is replaced by rapid, uncontrolled cell division and growth, which usually starts when a single cell goes out of control. Approximately one of every four Americans will develop some type of cancer during his or her lifetime. If detected early, many kinds of cancer can be treated, but tens of thousands of people still die each year from the disease.

Researchers believe that several different factors and combinations of factors are what cause cancer. One may be heredity, meaning that some people may inherit, within their genes, certain susceptibilities to cancer from their parents or other ancestors. Environmental factors are also often involved, including repeated exposure to heat, smoke, ultraviolet light and other kinds of radiation, and certain chemicals. There is overwhelming medical evidence, for example, that cigarette smoking causes lung cancer and that prolonged exposure to sunlight (which contains ultraviolet radiation) causes skin cancer. Another theory suggests that some unknown and noninfectious type of virus may be responsible for certain kinds of cancer. When they enter the body or strike its surface, these external factors may interact with the genes that carry a susceptibility to cancer, thereby triggering the disease.

Emphysema is a disease characterized by slow deterioration of the lungs, in which the tiny air sacs known as alveoli in the lungs lose their ordinary flexibility and rupture, thereby interfering with normal, efficient breathing. At present, no cure exists for emphysema, and doctors can only prescribe certain drugs and breathing aids to reduce the discomfort of the disease. Although emphysema can develop from asthma, bronchial infections, and other respiratory conditions, its primary cause is cigarette smoking. Studies show that smokers have a much higher risk of getting emphysema than do nonsmokers.

A satellite "map" of the ozone layer over the earth's Northern Hemisphere, looking straight down at the North Pole. Such mapping of the ozone layer has become more and more relevant, because pollutants released into the atmosphere are slowly eroding the layer, thereby exposing the earth to cancer-causing ultraviolet radiation from the sun.

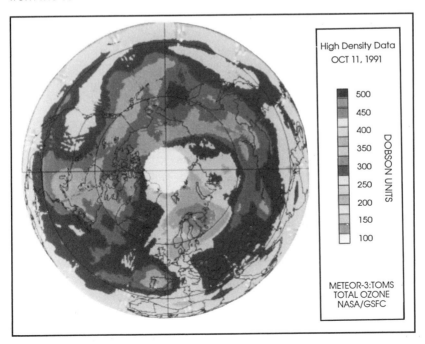

High Density Data
OCT 11, 1991

500
450
400
350   DOBSON UNITS
300
250
200
150
100

METEOR-3:TOMS
TOTAL OZONE
NASA/GSFC

Many noncommunicable diseases come from habits deeply entrenched in modern societies. Among such dangerous habits is a sedentary lifestyle, in which lack of exercise contributes to heart disease and other illnesses. Smoking adds to the risk of cancer and other illnesses; the excessive use of salt can cause or worsen high blood pressure; and the heavy use of sugar often leads to diabetes.

Diabetes and Heart Disease

Diabetes, a disturbance of body chemistry caused by the lack of an essential hormone called *insulin*, affects millions of people around the world. Typical symptoms of diabetes are fatigue and general weakness, weight loss even when food intake has not decreased, frequent urination, excessive thirst, and irritability.

Because of the body's deficiency of insulin, the cells of diabetic persons have trouble absorbing and breaking down glucose, a natural sugar derived from food that is an important source of energy for the body's various chemical processes. In diabetes, much of the sugar that should be absorbed by the cells instead accumulates in the bloodstream, increasing the concentration of sugar in the blood.

Although diabetes is inherited, not everyone who has a hereditary tendency toward developing it actually gets it. Those who actually do develop diabetes nearly always have too much sugar and other carbohydrates in their diets, are overweight, and get little or no exercise.

Diseases of the heart and arteries—especially coronary heart disease, which gradually obstructs the blood vessels that supply the heart itself—are major health problems in developed countries. This is because many of the factors contributing to these diseases are characteristic of modern, affluent societies. Among these factors are stress related to jobs and family factors, diets with an excessive content of saturated fats and cholesterol, tendencies toward overweight and obesity, lack of exercise, and the high frequency of smoking. Stress, excessive weight, and lack of exercise all contribute to heart disease by increasing the blood pressure and making the heart work harder. Smoking increases the heart rate and decreases the amount of oxygen that circulates through the blood for use by the body's tissues. Excess dietary fats lead to overweight, and cholesterol—a substance present in butter, meat, cheese, and many other fat-containing foods—accumulates on the insides of arteries, reducing their inner width and restricting the quantity of blood that flows through these vessels. If one of the main vessels leading to the heart becomes sufficiently blocked, a heart attack can result.

Similarly, too much salt in the diet can also be dangerous. This is because salt causes the body to retain fluids, some portion of which enter the blood and increase its volume. This increased volume of blood increases the pressure of the blood on the vessels through which the blood circulates, and can damage these vessels. The increased blood volume also forces the heart to work harder to pump the blood through the body, thereby weakening the heart and contributing to heart disease.

Reducing Risks

When it comes to noncommunicable diseases, practicing good hygiene means taking care of one's self and avoiding those habits and behaviors that are known to be detrimental to health. Taking care of one's self involves eating the right foods and getting regular exercise. Habits and behaviors to avoid are overeating, smoking, excessive consumption of alcohol, and any use of drugs. Clearly, doing these things does not absolutely guarantee that a person will not develop diabetes, cancer, heart disease, or other noncommunicable disease. But keeping the body fit and avoiding obvious health hazards greatly reduces the chances of developing such diseases. In other words, people should, to the best of their abilities, practice preventive medicine.

Certain types of cancer provide a good illustration of the way in which preventive medicine works. One of these is skin cancer, which

THE FALL OF A SPORTS HERO

The destructive effects of a drug such as cocaine on a person's health and life can be seen graphically in the rise and tragic fall of football star Larry Bethea, of Newport News, Virginia. Bright and talented, Bethea stood six feet five inches tall and weighed 220 pounds when still in high school. He was a good student who got along well with his teachers. While he was in college, playing football for Michigan State University, the Big Ten Conference named him its most valuable player. Then, in 1978, Bethea became the number one draft choice of the Dallas Cowboys professional football team. After receiving a six-figure bonus, he married his high school sweetheart, and his life seemed destined for continued success and happiness.

But for reasons no one could explain, Larry Bethea began using cocaine. By 1980, his storybook life had begun to crumble. Observing that his playing had become lackluster, his coaches benched him. Soon afterward, he started freebasing cocaine, smoking it through a pipe rather than inhaling the powder. His personal relationships suffered, and his wife finally pressed him for a divorce.

By 1986, Bethea was no longer able to play football and returned to Newport News to live with his mother. Within months, she had him arrested for stealing thousands of dollars from her, and although the judge suspended his sentence, it was clear that he would do anything to get money for drugs. On April 22, 1987, Bethea stole a handgun and robbed two convenience stores in his own neighborhood. The clerks immediately recognized him and telephoned police, who began looking for him. They found him the next morning, lying in a pool of blood near a local drug hangout. The hometown hero with a life and future most people only dream about had put the gun to his head and pulled the trigger.

is known to be caused by high doses of radiation from the sun and ultraviolet or infrared lamps. Consciously avoiding situations in which such radiation is excessive, such as prolonged sunbathing, automatically reduces the risk of developing skin cancer. The role of ultraviolet radiation in sunlight as a leading cause of skin cancer became an issue of special concern in the late 1980s and early 1990s, when scientists learned that various gases and industrial pollutants are damaging the ozone layer in the earth's atmosphere. Normally, this layer of ozone shields the earth from the sun's most dangerous ultraviolet rays. But as the ozone layer is destroyed by air pollution, the risk of skin cancer increases and occurs with minimal exposure to the sun.

Another example of preventative medicine is periodic monitoring of the body's systems to ensure that they are running smoothly. This means getting regular checkups by a doctor. For the person who is in good physical condition, a complete physical examination once a year is sufficient. People with specific problems or conditions, such as obesity, a history of heart problems, or diabetes, should get a checkup more often.

A good diet is essential to good health, and avoiding certain foods—such as those that contain excessive fat, salt, or sugar—greatly reduces the risks of specific noncommunicable diseases. Restricting the amount of sugar in the diet reduces the risk of developing diabetes, and staying away from foods rich in saturated fat and cholesterol helps control weight and reduces the risk of heart disease. Likewise, minimizing one's intake of salt or salty foods protects against high blood pressure. The importance of good eating habits will be discussed in more detail in chapter 7.

Exercise

One of the best preventive measures for maintaining good health is regular exercise. Normally, the older a person becomes, the greater is his or her risk of getting one or more noncommunicable diseases. But repeated study has proven that exercise and good physical conditioning greatly reduce the incidence of many noncommunicable diseases, especially those involving the heart and blood vessels. When someone exercises vigorously on a regular basis, his or her circulatory and respiratory systems work more strenuously than usual. As a result, the heart gradually becomes stronger, is able to pump more blood, and can therefore supply more oxygen to the tissues. Regular exercise also keeps the blood vessels and lungs in good working order, increasing their ability to work with the heart and muscles.

Health expert Kenneth Jones points out that in a person who does not exercise regularly, "The heart works harder, faster, and less efficiently" than it does in someone who is physically fit.

A person in good condition who is regularly active, observes Jones, may have a resting heart rate of 55 to 60 beats per minute, while a nonexerciser may have a resting heart rate of 70 beats per minute or more. This means that the nonexerciser forces his heart to beat nearly 30,000 more times each day—a considerable amount of extra work for every day, month, and year of life. Furthermore, although the heart of a fit person beats fewer times per day, it pumps a greater volume of blood, and the body responds by creating more blood vessels, es-

Regular exercise is an essential part of keeping the body in good physical condition and protecting it against heart disease and other noncommunicable illnesses. Exercise is beneficial even for very elderly persons and those whose mobility is limited by age or illness, such as this woman.

pecially in the muscles. This keeps the tissues alive and healthier for a much longer time than in someone who is not physically fit.

Regular exercise therefore results in continued good health as a person grows older. At one time, many people believed that it was one's chronologic age that determined his or her capacity for exercise. In other words, the older a person got, the less physical exercise it was thought he or she could perform. Doctors now know that this is not true. Not only can exercise keep the body working efficiently well into old age, but studies have repeatedly shown that people who are physically fit are healthier and better able to maintain their good health as they age. Today, science has shown that most people can engage in sensible and fairly vigorous exercise programs even into their seventies and eighties.

Avoiding Harmful Habits

Whereas exercise contributes to good health, such habits as smoking, drinking excessive quantities of alcohol, and taking drugs clearly damage one's health. Of these three practices, cigarette smoking is the leading cause of preventable illness and death in the Western Hemisphere. More than 300,000 people die of heart disease, lung cancer, and other smoking-related diseases each year in the United States alone. Besides containing solid pollutants, including cancer-causing tars and

Among the deadliest of human habits is cigarette smoking, which on a worldwide scale causes millions of deaths each year from cancer, heart disease, emphysema, and other noncommunicable diseases.

79

hydrocarbons, cigarette smoke contains nicotine, a highly poisonous alkaloid substance, and carbon monoxide, a toxic gas.

The most obvious damage done by smoking is to the lungs. Tobacco smoke and tar clog the air sacs in the lungs, reducing their capacity to inhale air and eliminate waste gases from the body and causing noticeable shortness of breath. As the smoking habit continues, the lungs can become increasingly irritated and scarred, resulting in emphysema. The heat, irritation, and perhaps other factors involved in the act of smoking can also trigger lung cancer. Any person who does smoke should quit as quickly as possible. Studies have shown that the lungs of people who have stopped smoking (and who have not already developed emphysema or lung cancer) slowly repair themselves, reducing the risk of serious disease. Unfortunately, quitting smoking is no easy task.

The nicotine in tobacco, besides being toxic, is also highly addictive. The best way to avoid the health hazards of smoking is therefore not to begin smoking in the first place.

Heavy and prolonged alcohol consumption is another leading cause of preventable noncommunicable illness. Alcohol depresses, or slows, the functions of the brain and nervous system. Studies have indicated that alcohol, when used infrequently and in moderate amounts, is relatively harmless to most people. The problem is that like tobacco, it is highly addictive and can easily lead one into the habit of drinking more alcohol more often.

Alcohol consumption can impair health in a number of ways. It can destroy the brain cells that control coordination and reflexes, and damage nerves in the arms, legs, and other parts of the body. Heavy use of alcohol weakens muscle tissue, causing the body to become progressively unfit and therefore contributing to declining health. One of the muscles that is weakened by repeated, heavy alcohol consumption is the heart. Moreover, drinking an unusually large amount of alcohol at one time can cause sudden heart failure. Every year there are dozens of reports of this happening to high school and college students who get involved in what they mistakenly think are harmless drinking contests. And besides affecting the heart and nervous system, heavy and prolonged use of alcohol leads to other noncom-

One way to reduce the risk of noncommunicable disease is to stop the habits that cause it. Breaking the smoking habit—often encouraged by mass "smokeouts" such as the one shown here—is an effective step toward better health.

municable illnesses, including stomach and intestinal ulcers and liver damage.

If good health is one's goal, recreational drugs of any kind should be avoided. After nicotine and alcohol, the two most commonly used recreational drugs are marijuana, or pot, and cocaine. Although some medical studies indicate that marijuana is not physically addictive, marijuana smoke is known to cause the same respiratory and circulatory damage that cigarette smoke causes. It is therefore a mistake to think that marijuana is a safe substitute for cigarettes. Cocaine, a stimulant that temporarily excites or speeds up many body functions, is highly addictive, as is crack, a very concentrated form of cocaine. Not only can cocaine cause an inability to sleep, known as insomnia, as well as ulcers and bleeding in the nasal cavity, but the heavy, prolonged use of cocaine damages the spinal cord, causing the user to suffer violent convulsions and making breathing difficult. Many people have died of cocaine overdoses.

Maintaining good health, then, is largely a matter of doing some things and not doing others. The things to do are to get regular medical checkups, eat the right foods, and exercise regularly. The things to avoid are those that create obvious risks of cancer, heart disease, and other noncommunicable diseases, such as prolonged exposure to sunlight, smoking, eating foods high in fat and cholesterol, and using destructive and addictive substances such as alcohol and cocaine.

CHAPTER 7

GOOD EATING HABITS

The Roman general Lucius Licinius Lucullus (117–58 B.C.) shown entertaining guests at his villa. Lucullus's tastes, famed for tending toward delicacies and rich foods, may be considered the converse of a properly balanced and nutritious diet.

Good eating habits are essential to ensuring a proper diet and nutrition. Unfortunately, many people are uninformed about such habits and how they affect nutrition. This is partly because the basics of what and how much to eat are not often taught in schools, and also because people are often misinformed by food advertising in the mass media. In advertising their products, food growers and manufacturers compete commercially for shares of the lucrative food market, appeal-

Although the past 75 years have seen a widespread improvement in the cleanliness of processed foods, they have not seen a comparable increase in the spread of responsible nutritional information.

ing to consumers' appetites by emphasizing how good their foods look and taste. Usually, as in the case of the many junk foods consumed each year, the poor nutritional value of many popular food products is underplayed or ignored. This is especially true for foods aimed at children, whose chief attraction to food is its taste. Children's television shows are often sponsored by companies who inundate young viewers with ads about sweet and sugary cereals, pastries, and other such questionable treats.

Adding to consumer confusion about what is or is not nutritious, food manufacturers often use misleading or ambiguous terms in listing the ingredients on their food packaging. Thus, a label that lists corn syrup, bleached flour, malt syrup, dextrose, fructose, and sugar as ingredients does not tell the entire story. Because sugar is listed last, it appears that there is little sugar in the product. But in reality, every one of the other ingredients in this food—except the flour—is a sugarlike substance. As a result, consumers who are not well-educated about nutrition often have difficulty in knowing whether the foods they buy and eat are really good for them.

Harmful Eating Patterns

Among other problems that result from poor eating habits in modern, affluent societies are obesity and anorexia. Among the factors contributing to the development of these problems are stress, depression, poor self-image, ignorance about nutrition, lack of exercise, and the distorted value that modern American society puts on thinness. This last factor is especially important. Because the fashion and film industries, as well as the media, constantly equate beauty with thinness, millions of people are obsessed with dieting. Unfortunately, the often unrealistic goals of dieting and the general lack of education about nutrition cause most diets to fail. Repeated unsuccessful attempts at dieting lead to harmful eating patterns that often end in serious health problems.

The most common eating problems are obesity, compulsive overeating, bulimia, and anorexia. The last three are referred to medically

A fast-food stand at Coney Island, New York. Although fast foods' appearance and taste may make them appealing, they do not provide a properly balanced diet, and if eaten too often they may hasten the development of heart disease and other illnesses.

as eating disorders and affect tens of millions of people in the United States and other Western countries. Each of these disorders has particular symptoms or signs, as well as types of behavior that distinguish it from the others, yet all three disorders are closely related. All of them are connected to the obsession with thinness and the dieting cycle. A common problem in all people with eating disorders is the fear of having a fat body. At one time or another, most persons who overeat tend to become fearful that they may become obese. Although the definition of obesity varies among medical authorities, it is a condition characterized by an excessive amount of adipose, or fatty, tissue. Most doctors agree that someone who is more than 20% above the ideal weight for a person of his or her height, type of body frame, and age is obese. Fear of obesity leads many people to begin destructive dieting cycles.

Binging and Purging

Persons who are constantly dieting in an attempt to lose weight deny themselves food when they really want to eat. Sooner or later they give in to this urge, and many of them engage in binge eating—the consumption of large amounts of tasty but nutritionally poor food in a very short time. Doctors have recently begun to call such people compulsive overeaters.

Compulsive overeaters usually binge at least twice a week for several months or more. During binges, they most often consume large quantities of sweets and highly caloric foods, such as ice cream, cakes, cookies, doughnuts, and potato chips. They may also eat cereals, hamburgers, or anything else that tastes good. The amounts of food eaten during binges can be enormous, for example: a gallon of ice cream, an entire cake, or two boxes of cereal with milk. Some binge eaters report consuming as many as 20,000 calories in a single sitting, the amount an average person eats in eight days.

After a few months of binging, compulsive overeaters often stop this behavior for a few weeks or months and go on diets, attempting to lose whatever weight they gained. After some or all of the weight is lost, they begin binging again. Thus, compulsive overeaters usually experience repeated weight changes of 10 to 20 pounds or more. There are also sufferers who binge several times a week, or even several times a day. Some of these people may eventually give up on dieting and become obese. Compulsive overeaters are both male and female. The exact number of people who suffer from the disorder is not known, but it could be in the tens of millions.

Sometimes, compulsive overeating can lead to the more serious disorder known as *bulimia*. Bulimics also regularly binge uncontrollably on large quantities of food. But unlike compulsive overeaters, who either try to diet or just accept being overweight, bulimics engage in the act of *purging*. Most often, this consists of vomiting up the food just eaten. Bulimics also use laxatives and diuretics to rid themselves of food. They engage in a regular routine of binging and purging, which usually occurs at least two or three times a week. Some bulimics binge and purge as often as several times a day. Almost always, bulimics are secretive about their binging and purging.

Bulimia has several harmful physical side effects. For one thing, when bulimics throw up, stomach acids come up with the vomit. Over the course of weeks or months, these acids can cause frequent sore throats, eat away at the enamel of the teeth, and make the mouth and jaw swell. Also, constant vomiting puts a great deal of stress on the stomach, often resulting in severe abdominal pains. Although both men and women can be bulimic, most who suffer from the disorder are female. There are no reliable figures for the number of bulimics but doctors' estimates range from 5% to 20% of the female population.

Self-Starvation

Many people are surprised to learn that *anorexia*, the disorder characterized by self-starvation, is closely related to the problems already described. Almost all anorexics, like people with other eating problems, begin by having trouble with excess weight. Some may gain only a few pounds. Others actually become obese. Either way, anorexic persons have an intense fear of becoming or remaining fat, and react by dieting.

TREATING EATING DISORDERS

Treating eating disorders is often a very difficult process. There are three important reasons for this. First, doctors still do not fully understand the causes of these disorders. Second, the effectiveness of any treatment is limited by many factors. These include: the individual personality and background of the patient, how much the patient cooperates in the treatment, the amount of support given by the patient's family and friends, the particular method of treatment chosen, and the sensitivity of the doctor. The third reason that eating disorders are so hard to treat is the importance of food. Because it is essential to life, people who abuse food cannot begin their treatment by eliminating the object of their obsession. They must instead learn to deal with food in a healthy manner, which can be very difficult.

The goal of every treatment for an eating disorder is the same: to have the subject learn to deal with food in a normal, healthy way. Recovery means achieving ordered rather than disordered eating habits. Because every case is different, doctors have found that the same method or combination of methods that helps one patient may not help another.

One of the most common treatments for eating disorders, especially for anorexia, is hospitalization. In a hospital setting, doctors, nurses, and relatives of the patient all work to rehabilitate the patient's self-image and help him or her reach a healthy weight. Another treatment involves drug therapy. In cases where the eating disorder is highly motivated by depression, doctors may use antidepressant drugs to help reduce or eliminate the state of depression.

In another approach to treatment called behavior modification, doctor and patient work together to eliminate old harmful beliefs and life-style routines that contributed to the disorder and establish new, healthier eating habits. Counseling therapy also attempts to institute better eating habits by identifying the causes of the person's eating problem.

Unlike compulsive overeaters, however, anorexics diet so severely that they literally starve themselves. Most anorexics consume only about 200 to 500 calories a day, perhaps one-fifth or less of the amount eaten by an average person. Because they eat so little, they lose a great deal of weight. But although they reject food, they still strongly desire it, and many anorexics occasionally binge. They may eat large amounts of highly caloric, easily digestible foods such as ice cream, cookies, or sour cream. Like compulsive overeaters, they hope to prevent any weight gain by continued dieting.

Anorexic behavior is extremely harmful, both physically and mentally. As anorexics eat less and less, their bodies burn more and more of their fatty tissues. Eventually, nearly all of the fatty tissues in their bodies are gone. But their bodies still require nutrients in order to continue functioning, so they begin to burn and deplete their muscle tissues, and their weight may eventually drop to 70 pounds or less. Nearly all persons who suffer from anorexia are female. Doctors are still uncertain about the number of anorexics in society, but estimate that 1% of the female population is anorexic.

Obviously, people who are battling with obesity, compulsive overeating, bulimia, or anorexia find it difficult to develop a good sense of hygiene regarding food. Those who suffer with these serious problems should not attempt to deal with them on their own. Instead, they should consult a doctor and rigidly follow any prescribed treatment (see sidebar on page 88). People who do not suffer with these problems and want to avoid them should not attempt to diet on their own, but rather should diet only under a doctor's supervision. They should educate themselves about nutrition and develop a sensible approach to eating. The following is a simple guide to healthy eating habits, based on sound advice from doctors and dieticians.

Knowing When To Eat

Eating right is partly a matter of *how much* to eat and partly a matter of *what* to eat. The amount of food that a person needs each day to maintain normal health is called the daily calorie requirement. *Calories* are a measure of the amount of heat energy burned by the body. Foods are said to "contain" calories because a certain number of calories will be burned when these foods are eaten. The number of calories required varies from one person to another, depending on such factors as gender, body size, and level of physical activity. To find out how many calories are needed each day, a person should consult a doctor or nutritionist.

It is important to stress that regularly consuming one's daily calorie requirement does *not* mean counting or worrying about the number of calories consumed. The body instinctively knows how much food it needs, and signals that need by creating a feeling of hunger. Simply eating when hungry and stopping when the feeling of hunger is gone will ensure the appropriate calorie intake.

A consumer at the first American pizza stand in Moscow, Russia. The spread of fast foods, with their failure to provide balanced nutrition, may export nutritional problems from the more advanced to the less developed nations of the world.

Members of a 4-H Club caring for a young dairy cow. Modern technologies make it possible to eliminate much of the unhealthy saturated fat from milk and other dairy products, while leaving them with the protein, calcium, and other essential nutrients they have always contained.

This approach to regulating the amount of food eaten is the healthiest alternative to a reducing diet. A person who is moderately overweight, for instance, who eats only when hungry will eventually reach his or her ideal weight, although it will usually take time. Weight loss will be very slow as the body readjusts to its healthy state, and the person may lose only a pound or less every month. The important thing is that the person will get used to eating in a healthy manner and be less likely to gain the weight back. Furthermore, he or she will not feel deprived of food, thereby reducing the chances of developing harmful eating patterns and disorders.

Knowing What To Eat

In addition to eating the right amount of food, proper nutrition also includes knowing which foods are best. To maintain healthy functioning, the body needs certain nutrients every day, the three most basic being proteins, carbohydrates, and fats. Proteins are the building blocks that the body uses to make skin, muscle tissue, and other body parts. The body uses fats as a source of energy and vitamins. Carbohydrates are also important energy sources, and in addition provide many essential vitamins and minerals. The body works best when it gets these three nutrients in certain proportions. According to dietary experts, the healthiest diet for an average person contains about 15% proteins, 35% fats, and 50% carbohydrates. People who are unusually active may need a higher proportion of carbohydrates, and athletes building muscle mass need a higher proportion of protein. It is best to consult a doctor or nutritionist about what proportion of nutrients is healthiest for you. Proteins are found in meats, fish and other seafoods, and dairy products, including milk, cheese, and yogurt. Plants contain proteins too, but in smaller amounts. That is why people who eat vegetarian diets can still receive the correct amounts of protein.

Fats also come from animal products, such as meat and milk, as well as from plants. Some fats are less healthy than others. Fats that come from red meat and dairy products are called high-density, or saturated, fats. Those from plants and white meats such as chicken and fish, are called low-density, or less-saturated, fats. The body has a much harder time dealing with saturated fats, which contribute to heart disease and other problems. Therefore, it is healthier to get into the habit of eating more foods that contain less-saturated fats and fewer foods with saturated fats.

Carbohydrates are made up of sugars. Some of these are simple sugars, such as the sugar known as sucrose, which is found in candy bars, frostings, and honey. These have little or no nutritional value. Other sugars are more complex and are therefore referred to as complex carbohydrates, or starches. These are vital to the body because many of them can be broken down in the body to yield simple sugars to meet the body's energy needs or which can be reassembled into other carbohydrates that can be stored in the body to be broken down and used as needed. Grains, breads, pasta, beans, and potatoes are rich in complex carbohydrates.

Some of the sources listed at the back of this book provide a more detailed discussion of nutrition. Anyone who is unsure about what to eat or worried about weight gain or loss should discuss these concerns with a doctor or nutritionist. Remember that eating right is just as important as all of the other precautions relating to hygiene discussed in this book. A healthy diet, in combination with regular exercise, clean personal habits and living conditions, and the avoidance of obvious health risks is the best approach to a lifetime of good health.

APPENDIX

FOR MORE INFORMATION

The following is a list of organizations that can provide further information on the issues discussed in this book.

AIDS

AIDS Hotline for Teens
(800) 234-TEEN

Canadian AIDS Society
100 Sparks Street, Suite 701
Ottawa, Ontario K1P 5B7
Canada
(613) 230-3580

The Centers for Disease Control
National AIDS Hotline
(800) 342-AIDS (24 hours a day, 7 days a week)

National AIDS Information
Clearinghouse
(800) 458-5231

CANCER

American Cancer Society
1599 Clifton Road NE
Atlanta, GA 30329
(404) 320-3333

Canadian Cancer Society
10 Alcorn Avenue, Suite 200
Toronto, Ontario M4V 3B1
Canada
(416) 961-7223

National Cancer Institute
National Institutes of Health
4000 Rockville Pike
Building 31, 10A24
Bethesda, MD 20892
(301) 496-5583

EATING DISORDERS

Anorexia Nervosa and Related Eating
Disorders, Inc. (ANRED)
P.O. Box 5102
Eugene, OR 97405
(503) 344-1144

Weight Loss/Behavior Modification
Program for Teens Shapedown
Balboa Publishing
11 Library Place
San Anselmo, CA 94960
(415) 453-8886

ENVIRONMENTAL AGEN-CIES/ORGANIZATIONS

Center for Environmental Information
33 South Washington Street
Rochester, NY 14608
(716) 546-3796

United Nations Environment Program
Room DC 2-0803
United Nations
New York, NY 10017
(212) 963-8093

U.S. Environmental Protection
 Agency (EPA)
401 M Street SW
Washington, DC 20460
(202) 382-2080

Worldwatch Institute
1776 Massachusetts Avenue NW
Washington, DC 20036
(202) 452-1999

EXERCISE

Aerobics and Fitness Association of
 America
15250 Ventura Blvd., Suite 310
Sherman Oaks, CA 91403
(818) 905-0040

Canadian Association for Health,
 Physical Education, and Recreation
1600 James Naismith Drive, Suite 606
Gloucester, Ontario K1B 5N4
Canada
(613) 748-5622

President's Council on Physical
 Fitness and Sports
701 Pennsylvania Avenue, Suite 250
Washington, DC 20004
(202) 272-3421

HEART DISEASE

Canadian Heart Foundation
160 George Street, Suite 200
Ottawa, Ontario K1N 9M2
Canada
(613) 237-4361

National Heart, Lung, and Blood
 Institute
National Institutes of Health
9000 Rockville Pike
 Building 31, Room 4A21
Bethesda, MD 20892
(301) 496-4236

NUTRITION

Food and Drug Administration
Office of Consumer Affairs
5600 Fishers Lane, HFE-88
Rockville, MD 20857
(301) 443-3170

Food and Nutrition Information
 Center
National Agricultural Library
Room 304
Beltsville, MD 20705
(301) 344-3719

National Institute of Nutrition
1565 Carling Avenue, Suite 400
Ottawa, Ontario K1Z 8R1
Canada
(613) 725-1889

U.S. Department of Agriculture
Food Safety and Inspection Service
Washington, DC 20250
Meat and Poultry Hotline:
(800) 447-3333 (in Washington, DC)
(800) 535-4555 (outside Washington,
 DC)

PREVENTION OF INFECTIOUS DISEASES

Centers for Disease Control
Department of Health and Human
  Services
Public Health Service
Atlanta, GA 30333
(404) 639-3311

National Institute of Allergy and
  Infectious Diseases
  (NIAID/NIH)
9000 Rockville Pike
Building 31, Room 7A32
Bethesda, MD 20892
(301) 496-5717

Office of Disease Prevention and
  Health Promotion
National Health Information
  Center
P.O. Box 1133
Washington, DC 20013-1133
(800) 565-4167 (in Maryland)
(800) 336-4797 (outside Maryland)

U.S. Public Health Service
General Information Hotline:
  (800) 342-2437

World Health Organization (WHO)
20 Avenue Appia
1211 Geneva 27,
Switzerland

SEXUALLY TRANSMITTED DISEASES

American Foundation for the Prevention of Venereal Disease, Inc.
799 Broadway, Suite 638
New York, NY 10003
(212) 759-2069

American Venereal Disease
  Association
5222 Balboa Avenue, Suite 52
San Diego, CA 92117
(619) 565-2439

National Sexually Transmitted Disease
  Hotline
(800) 227-8922

Planned Parenthood
380 Second Avenue, 3rd Floor
New York, NY 10010
(212) 274-7200
(212) 541-7800 (for national
  information)
(provides information on basic
  gynecological care, birth control,
  abortion, pregnancy, and childbirth)

WATER POLLUTION

Clean Water Action
1320 18th Street NW, Suite 300
Washington, DC 20036
(202) 457-0336

Pollution Probe
12 Madison Avenue
Toronto, Ontario M5R 2S1
Canada
(416) 926-1907

FURTHER READING

Aylesworth, Thomas G. *The World of Microbes*. New York: Franklin Watts, 1975.

Brody, Jane. *Jane Brody's Nutrition Book*. New York: Bantam Books, 1977.

Cantrell, Alan. *AIDS: The Mystery and the Solution*. Los Angeles: Aries Rising Press, 1986.

Davies, Bruce, and David Ashton. *Why Exercise?* New York: Blackwell, 1986.

Dolan, Edward F. *Drugs in Sports*. New York: Franklin Watts, 1986.

Drews, Frederick R., et al. *A Healthy Life: Exercise, Behavior, Nutrition*. Indianapolis: Benchmark Press, 1986.

Erlinger, Ellen. *Eating Disorders*. Minneapolis: Lerner, 1988.

Galperin, Anne. *Stroke and Heart Disease*. New York: Chelsea House, 1991.

Gibson, John. *Health: Personal and Communal*. London: Faber and Faber, 1959.

Hirschmann, Jane R., and Carol H. Munter. *Overcoming Overeating*. New York: Fawcett Columbine, 1988.

Jaret, Peter. "The Disease Detectives." *National Geographic*, January 1991.

Jones, Kenneth L., et al. *Dimensions: A Changing Concept of Health.* San Francisco: Canfield Press, 1974.

Meyer, Ernest A. *Microorganisms and Human Disease.* New York: Prentice-Hall, 1974.

O'Conner, Karen. *Garbage.* San Diego: Lucent Books, 1989.

O'Neill, Cherry Boone. *Starving for Attention.* New York: Dell, 1982.

Schmid, Ronald F. *Traditional Foods Are Your Best Medicine.* Stratford, CT: Ocean View, 1987.

Stuller, Jay. "Cleanliness Has Only Recently Become a Virtue." *Smithsonian,* February 1991.

Wagman, Richard J., ed. *The New Concise Family Health & Medical Guide.* Chicago: Ferguson, 1971.

GLOSSARY

acquired immune deficiency syndrome (AIDS) an acquired defect in the immune system caused by the HIV virus and spread by blood or sexual contact

algae unicellular aquatic organisms that are usually not disease causing

anorexia nervosa an eating disorder characterized by the fear of eating or gaining weight

bacteria unicellular organisms that lack a distinct nuclear membrane

binge a period of uncontrolled overeating

bulimia an eating disorder characterized by frequent binging and purging of food

calorie a measure of the amount of heat energy used by the body to burn foods

cancer a disease marked by malignant tumors that destroy normal tissue as it spreads to adjacent tissue layers or to other parts of the body

chlamydia a series of sexually transmitted infections caused by different strains of the bacterium *Chlamydia trachomatis*

communicable disease also known as infectious disease; a disease caused by germs that can be spread from one person to another

compulsive overeating an eating disorder characterized by frequent binging of food

contraceptives devices that prevent pregnancy

diabetes an abnormal condition in which the body cannot metabolize sugar

emphysema a disease characterized by the slow deterioration of the lungs, in which the alveoli lose their ordinary flexibility, preventing normal, efficient breathing

epidemiology the systematic study of the incidence, distribution, and control of disease in a population

filtration a water purification method in which water is forced through sand and gravel to remove bacteria and other impurities

fission a splitting or breaking up into parts

fungi parasitic plants such as mushrooms and yeasts

genital warts condyloma; fleshy growths occurring in and around the genitals and anus in both sexes; transmitted sexually by the human papilloma virus

germ theory the doctrine that communicable diseases are caused by germs

gonorrhea bacterially caused venereal disease that affects the genital mucous membranes; if treated early, antibiotics can be effective; if left untreated, serious complications may occur

herpes simplex an STD caused by a viral infection; causes a painful sore or sores to appear usually on the mouth or anus and genitals; can recur throughout a person's life

hygiene the application of science to the preservation of good health and the prevention of disease

insulin a hormone secreted in response to elevated levels of glucose in the blood

landfill method of garbage disposal in which the refuse is placed between layers of earth to build up low-lying land

menstruation the cyclic shedding of the uterine lining that occurs in the absence of pregnancy during the reproductive period (puberty through menopause) of the female

microbiology the study of microscopic creatures, including germs

microorganisms tiny living cells that cannot be seen with the naked eye; germs

mitosis cell division of somatic cells in which each daughter cell contains the same number of chromosomes as did the parent cell

monogamous having one mate or sexual partner exclusively for a period of time

noncommunicable disease also known as noninfectious disease; a disease that occurs within an individual and which cannot spread to others

nucleus the area in a cell in which genetic material is found; an essential agent in the growth and reproduction of a cell

obesity a bodily condition in which there is an excess of fat in relation to other body components; a person is considered to be obese when he or she is 20% or more over the ideal weight

ozone a colorless gas, structurally similar to but heavier than oxygen; in the upper atmosphere it forms a layer that protects the earth's surface from dangerous ultraviolet radiation; ozone that builds up in the lower atmosphere contributes to air pollution

parasite a living creature, usually small, that enters the body and lives off the body's tissues and nutrients

photochemical smog air pollution made up primarily of ozone and nitrous and sulfur dioxides

photosynthesis the process by which plants take in carbon dioxide and water and use them to produce oxygen and the carbohydrates that enable them to grow

primary treatment the first step in sewage treatment in which the liquid and solid parts of sewage are separated

protozoans small organisms with relatively complex internal structures; larger than bacteria

purge the evacuation of food from the body, either by the use of laxatives or by vomiting

recycling saving and reusing certain kinds of refuse, such as glass bottles, plastics, and paper products

secondary treatment the second step in sewage treatment, in which bacteria consume the sewage, altering its chemical makeup

sewage a mixture of water and solid waste materials

sexually transmitted diseases (STDs) infectious diseases that pass from one person to another during sexual contact, including AIDS, gonorrhea, syphillis, and genital warts

toxins poisonous substances produced by plants or animals

transfer station a facility to which people take their trash and garbage; from there the refuse is taken elsewhere for treatment, incineration, recycling, or inclusion in a landfill

vaccine a substance made of a killed or weakened bacterium or virus; stimulates the body to create antibodies that increase an individual's immunity to a particular disease

viruses tiny noncellular germs that invade and live off of living cells

yeasts fungal germs that reproduce by releasing spores

INDEX

PICTURE CREDITS

Don Nardo is an actor, filmmaker, and composer, as well as an award-winning writer. He has written articles, short stories, more than 30 books, and also screenplays and teleplays, including work for Warner Bros. and ABC television. He has appeared in dozens of stage productions and has worked in front of or behind the camera in more than 20 films. His musical compositions, such as his oratorio *Richard III*, and his film score for a version of *The Time Machine*, have been played by regional orchestras. Mr. Nardo lives with his wife, Christine, on Cape Cod, Massachusetts.

Dale C. Garell, M.D., is medical director of California Children Services, Department of Health Services, County of Los Angeles. He is also associate dean for curriculum at the University of Southern California School of Medicine and clinical professor in the Department of Pediatrics & Family Medicine at the University of Southern California School of Medicine. From 1963 to 1974, he was medical director of the Division of Adolescent Medicine at Children's Hospital in Los Angeles. Dr. Garell has served as president of the Society for Adolescent Medicine, chairman of the youth committee of the American Academy of Pediatrics, and as a forum member of the White House Conference on Children (1970) and White House Conference on Youth (1971). He has also been a member of the editorial board of the *American Journal of Diseases of Children.*

C. Everett Koop, M.D., Sc.D., is former Surgeon General, deputy assistant secretary for health, and director of the Office of International Health of the U.S. Public Health Service. A pediatric surgeon with an international reputation, he was previously surgeon-in-chief of Children's Hospital of Philadelphia and professor of pediatric surgery and pediatrics at the University of Pennsylvania. Dr. Koop is the author of more than 175 articles and books on the practice of medicine. He has served as surgery editor of the *Journal of Clinical Pediatrics* and editor-in-chief of the *Journal of Pediatric Surgery*. Dr. Koop has received nine honorary degrees and numerous other awards, including the Denis Brown Gold Medal of the British Association of Paediatric Surgeons, the William E. Ladd Gold Medal of the American Academy of Pediatrics, and the Copernicus Medal of the Surgical Society of Poland. He is a chevalier of the French Legion of Honor and a member of the Royal College of Surgeons, London.